GEORGE
MACDONALD

BOOKS BY C. S. LEWIS

A Grief Observed
George MacDonald: An Anthology
Mere Christianity
Miracles
The Abolition of Man
The Great Divorce
The Problem of Pain
The Screwtape Letters (with *"Screwtape Proposes a Toast"*)
The Weight of Glory

ALSO AVAILABLE FROM HARPERCOLLINS

The Chronicles of Narnia:
The Magician's Nephew
The Lion, the Witch and the Wardrobe
The Horse and His Boy
Prince Caspian
The Voyage of the Dawn Treader
The Silver Chair
The Last Battle

GEORGE
MACDONALD

AN ANTHOLOGY
365 READINGS

EDITED AND WITH A PREFACE BY

C. S. Lewis

HarperOne
An Imprint of HarperCollinsPublishers

HarperOne

GEORGE MACDONALD: *An Anthology*. Copyright © 1946 by C. S. Lewis Pte. Ltd. Copyright renewed 1973 C. S. Lewis Pte. Ltd.

HarperCollins books may be purchased for educational, business, or sales promotional use. For information please e-mail the Special Markets Department at SPsales@harpercollins.com.

HarperCollins Web site: http://www.harpercollins.com

HarperCollins®, 📖®, and HarperOne™ are trademarks of HarperCollins Publishers.

FIRST HARPERCOLLINS PAPERBACK EDITION PUBLISHED IN 2001

Library of Congress Cataloging-in-Publication Data
MacDonald, 1824–1905.
[Selections. 2001]
George MacDonald : an anthology : 365 readings / edited and with
a preface by C. S. Lewis.
p. cm.
Originally published: New York : Simon & Schuster, 1996
Includes bibliographical references.
ISBN 978-0-06-065319-4
1. MacDonald, George, 1824–1905—Quotations. 2. Christian
life—Quotations, maxims, etc. 3. Christian life—Meditations.
I. Lewis, C. S. (Clive Staples), 1898–1963. II. Title.
PR4966.L4   2001
823'.8—dc21   00-063226

23 24 25 26 27 LBC 32 31 30 29 28

To Mary Neylan

Contents

CONTENTS

CONTENTS

CONTENTS

CONTENTS

CONTENTS

PREFACE

All that I know of George MacDonald I have learned either from his own books or from the biography (*George MacDonald and His Wife*) which his son, Dr. Greville MacDonald, published in 1924; nor have I ever, but once, talked of him to anyone who had met him. For the very few facts which I am going to mention I am therefore entirely dependent on Dr. MacDonald.

We have learned from Freud and others about those distortions in character and errors in thought which result from a man's early conflicts with his father. Far the most important thing we can know about George MacDonald is that his whole life illustrates the opposite process. An almost perfect relationship with his father was the earthly root of all his wisdom. From his own father, he said, he first learned that Fatherhood must be at the core of the universe. He was thus prepared in an unusual way to teach that religion in which the relation of Father and Son is of all relations the most central.

His father appears to have been a remarkable man — a man hard, and tender, and humorous all at once, in the old fashion of Scotch Christianity. He had had his leg cut off above the knee in the days before chloroform, refusing the customary dose of preliminary whisky, and "only for one moment, when the knife first transfixed the flesh, did he turn his face away and ejaculate a faint, sibilant *whiff*." He had quelled with a fantastic joke at his own expense an ugly riot in which he was being burned in effigy. He forbade his son to touch a saddle until he had learned to ride well without one. He advised him "to give over the fruitless game of poetry." He asked from him, and obtained, a promise to renounce tobacco at the age of twenty-three. On the other hand he objected to grouse shooting on the score of cruelty and had in general a tenderness for animals not very usual among farmers more than a hundred years ago; and his son reports that he never, as boy or man, asked him for anything without getting what he asked. Doubtless this tells us as much about the son's character as the father's and should be taken in connection with our extract on prayer (104). "He who seeks the Father more than anything He can give, is likely to have what he asks, for he is not likely to ask amiss." The theological maxim is rooted in the experiences of the author's childhood. This is what may be called the "anti-Freudian predicament" in operation.

George MacDonald's family (though hardly his father) were of course Calvinists. On the intellectual side his history is largely a history of escape from the

theology in which he had been brought up. Stories of
such emancipation are common in the nineteenth cen-
tury; but George MacDonald's story belongs to this
familiar pattern only with a difference. In most such
stories the emancipated person, not content with repu-
diating the doctrines, comes also to hate the persons, of
his forebears, and even the whole culture and way of
life with which they are associated. Thus books like
The Way of All Flesh come to be written; and later gen-
erations, if they do not swallow the satire wholesale as
history, at least excuse the author for a one-sidedness
which a man in his circumstances could hardly have
been expected to avoid. Of such personal resentment I
find no trace in MacDonald. It is not we who have to
find extenuating circumstances for his point of view.
On the contrary, it is he himself, in the very midst of his
intellectual revolt, who forces us, whether we will or
no, to see elements of real and perhaps irreplaceable
worth in the thing from which he is revolting.

All his life he continued to love the rock from which
he had been hewn. All that is best in his novels carries
us back to that "kaleyard" world of granite and
heather, of bleaching greens beside burns that look as if
they flowed not with water but with stout, to the thud-
ding of wooden machinery, the oatcakes, the fresh
milk, the pride, the poverty, and the passionate love of

hard-won learning. His best characters are those which reveal how much real charity and spiritual wisdom can coexist with the profession of a theology that seems to encourage neither. His own grandmother, a truly terrible old woman who had burnt his uncle's fiddle as a Satanic snare, might well have appeared to him as what is now (inaccurately) called "a mere sadist." Yet when something very like her is delineated in *Robert Falconer* and again in *What's Mine's Mine,* we are compelled to look deeper—to see, inside the repellent crust, something that we can wholeheartedly pity and even, with reservations, respect. In this way MacDonald illustrates, not the doubtful maxim that to know all is to forgive all, but the unshakeable truth that to forgive is to know. He who loves, sees.

He was born in 1824 at Huntly in Aberdeenshire and entered King's College at Aberdeen in 1840. In 1842 he spent some months in the North of Scotland cataloguing the library of a great house which has never been identified. I mention the fact because it made a lifelong impression on MacDonald. The image of a great house seen principally from the library and always through the eyes of a stranger or a dependent (even Mr. Vane in *Lilith* never seems at home in the library which is called his) haunts his books to the end. It is therefore reasonable to suppose that the "great house in the

North" was the scene of some important crisis or development in his life. Perhaps it was here that he first came under the influence of German Romanticism.

In 1850 he received what is technically known as a "Call" to become the Minister of a dissenting chapel in Arundel. By 1852 he was in trouble with the "deacons" for heresy, the charges being that he had expressed belief in a future state of probation for heathens and that he was tainted with German theology. The deacons took a roundabout method to be rid of him, by lowering his salary—it had been £150 a year and he was now married—in the hope that this would induce him to resign. But they had misjudged their man. MacDonald merely replied that this was bad enough news for him but that he supposed he must try to live on less. And for some time he continued to do so, often helped by the offerings of his poorest parishioners who did not share the views of the more prosperous Deacons. In 1853, however, the situation became impossible. He resigned and embarked on the career of lecturing, tutoring, occasional preaching, writing, and "odd jobs" which was his lot almost to the end. He died in 1905.

His lungs were diseased and his poverty was very great. Literal starvation was sometimes averted only by those last moment deliverances which agnostics attribute to chance and Christians to Providence. It is against this background of reiterated failure and incessant peril that some of the following extracts can be most profitably read. His resolute condemnations of anxiety come from one who has a right to speak; nor does their tone encourage the theory that they owe anything to the pathological wishful thinking—the *spes phthisica*—of the consumptive. None of the evidence suggests such a character. His peace of mind came not from building on the future but from resting in what he called "the holy Present." His resignation to poverty (see Number 274) was at the opposite pole from that of the stoic. He appears to have been a sunny, playful man, deeply appreciative of all really beautiful and delicious things that money can buy, and no less deeply content to do without them. It is perhaps significant— it is certainly touching—that his chief recorded weakness was a Highland love of finery; and he was all his life hospitable as only the poor can be.

In making these extracts I have been concerned with MacDonald not as a writer but as a Christian teacher. If I were to deal with him as a writer, a man of letters, I should be faced with a difficult critical problem. If we define Literature as an art whose medium is words, then certainly MacDonald has no place in its first rank—perhaps not even in its second. There are indeed passages, many of them in this collection, where the wisdom and (I would dare to call it) the holiness that are in him triumph over and even burn away the baser elements in his style: the expression becomes precise, weighty, economic; acquires a cutting edge. But he does not maintain this level for long. The texture of his writing as a whole is undistinguished, at times fumbling. Bad pulpit traditions cling to it; there is sometimes a nonconformist verbosity, sometimes an old Scotch weakness for florid ornament (it runs right through them from Dunbar to the Waverly Novels), sometimes an oversweetness picked up from Novalis. But this does not quite dispose of him even for the literary critic. What he does best is fantasy—fantasy that hovers between the allegorical and the mythopoeic. And this, in my opinion, he does better than any man. The critical problem with which we are confronted is whether this art—the art of myth-making—is a species of the literary art. The objection to so classifying it is that the Myth does not essentially exist in *words* at all. We all agree that the story of Balder is a great myth, a thing of inexhaustible value. But of whose version— whose *words*—are we thinking when we say this?

For my own part, the answer is that I am not thinking of anyone's words. No poet, as far as I know or can remember, has told this story supremely well. I am not thinking of any particular version of it. If the story is anywhere embodied in words, that is almost an accident. What really delights and nourishes me is a particular pattern of events, which would equally delight and nourish if it had reached me by some medium which involved no words at all—say by a mime, or a film. And I find this to be true of all such stories. When I think of the story of the Argonauts and praise it, I am not praising Apollonius Rhodius (whom I never finished) nor Kingsley (whom I have forgotten) nor even Morris, though I consider his version a very pleasant poem. In this respect stories of the mythical type are at the opposite pole from lyrical poetry. If you try to take the "theme" of Keats's *Nightingale* apart from the very words in which he has embodied it, you find that you are talking about almost nothing. Form and content can there be separated only by a false abstraction. But in a myth—in a story where the mere pattern of events is all that matters—this is not so. Any means of communication whatever which succeeds in lodging those events in our imagination has, as we say, "done the trick." After that you can throw the means of communication away. To be sure, if the means of communication are words, it is desirable that a letter which brings you important news should be fairly written. But this is only a minor convenience; for the letter will, in any case, go into the wastepaper basket as soon as you have mastered its contents, and the words (those of Lemprière would have done) are going to be forgotten as soon as you have mastered the Myth. In poetry the words are the body and the "theme" or "content" is the soul. But in myth the imagined events are the body and something inexpressible is the soul: the words, or mime, or film, or pictorial series are not even clothes— they are not much more than a telephone. Of this I had evidence some years ago when I first heard the story of Kafka's *Castle* related in conversation and afterwards read the book for myself. The reading added nothing. I had already received the myth, which was all that mattered.

Most myths were made in prehistoric times, and, I suppose, not consciously made by individuals at all. But every now and then there occurs in the modern world a genius—a Kafka or a Novalis—who can make such a story. MacDonald is the greatest genius of this kind whom I know. But I do not know how to classify such genius. To call it literary genius seems unsatisfactory since it can coexist with great inferiority in the art of words—nay, since its connection with words at all turns out to be merely external and, in a sense, accidental. Nor can it be fitted into any of the other arts. It begins to look as if there were an art, or a gift, which criticism has largely ignored. It may even be one of the greatest arts; for it produces works which give us (at the first meeting) as much delight and (on prolonged acquaintance) as much wisdom and strength as the works of the greatest poets. It is in some ways more akin to music than to poetry — or at least to most poetry. It goes beyond the expression of things we have already felt. It arouses in us sensations we have never had before, never anticipated having, as though we had broken out of our normal mode of consciousness and "possessed joys not promised to our birth." It gets under our skin, hits us at a level deeper than our thoughts or even our passions, troubles oldest certainties till all questions are reopened, and in general shocks us more fully awake than we are for most of our lives.

It was in this mythopoeic art that MacDonald excelled. And from this it follows that his best art is least represented in this collection. The great works are *Phantastes,* the *Curdie* books, *The Golden Key, The Wise Woman,* and *Lilith.* From them, just because they are supremely good in their own kind, there is little to be extracted. The meaning, the suggestion, the radiance, is incarnate in the whole story: it is only by chance that you find any detachable merits. The novels, on the other hand, have yielded me a rich crop. This does not mean that they are good novels. Necessity made MacDonald a novelist, but few of his novels are good and none is very good. They are best when they depart most from the canons of novel writing, and that in two directions. Sometimes they depart in order to come nearer to fantasy, as in the whole character of the hero in *Sir Gibbie* or the opening chapters of *Wilfred Cumbermede*. Sometimes they diverge into direct and prolonged preachments which would be intolerable if a man were reading for the story, but which are in fact welcome because the author, though a poor novelist, is a supreme preacher. Some of his best things are thus hidden in his dullest books: my task here has been almost one of exhumation. I am speaking so far of the novels as I think they would appear if judged by any reasonably objective standard. But it is, no doubt, true that any reader who loves holiness and loves MacDonald—yet perhaps he will need to love Scotland too—can find even in the worst of them something that disarms criticism and will come to feel a queer, awkward charm in their very faults. (But that, of course, is what happens to us with all favorite authors.) One rare, and all but unique, merit these novels must be allowed. The "good" characters are always the best and most convincing. His saints live; his villains are stagey.

This collection, as I have said, was designed not to revive MacDonald's literary reputation but to spread his religious teaching. Hence most of my extracts are taken from the three volumes of *Unspoken Sermons.* My own debt to this book is almost as great as one man can owe to another: and nearly all serious inquirers to whom I have introduced it acknowledge that it has given them great help—sometimes indispensable help toward the very acceptance of the Christian faith.

I will attempt no historical or theological classification of MacDonald's thought, partly because I have not the learning to do so, still more because I am no great friend to such pigeonholing. One very effective way of silencing the voice of conscience is to impound in an *Ism* the teacher through whom it speaks: the trumpet no longer seriously disturbs our rest when we have murmured "Thomist," "Barthian," or "Existentialist." And in MacDonald it is always the voice of conscience that speaks. He addresses the will: the demand for obedience, for "something to be neither more nor less nor other than *done*" is incessant. Yet in that very voice of conscience every other faculty somehow speaks as well—intellect, and imagination, and humor, and fancy, and all the affections; and no man in modern times was perhaps more aware of the distinction between Law and Gospel, the inevitable failure of mere morality. The Divine Sonship is the key-conception which unites all the different elements of his thought. I dare not say that he is never in error; but to speak plainly I know hardly any other writer who seems to be closer, or more continually close, to the Spirit of Christ Himself. Hence his Christlike union of tenderness and severity. Nowhere else outside the New Testament have I found terror and comfort so intertwined. The title "Inexorable Love" which I have given to several individual extracts would serve for the whole collection. Inexorability—but never the inexorability of anything less than love—runs through it like a refrain; "escape is hopeless"—"agree quickly with your adversary"—"compulsion waits behind"—"the uttermost farthing will be exacted." Yet this urgency never becomes shrill. All the sermons are suffused with a spirit of love and wonder which prevents it from doing so. MacDonald shows God threatening, but (as Jeremy Taylor says) "He threatens terrible things if we will not be happy."

In many respects MacDonald's thought has, in a high degree, just those excellences which his period and his personal history would lead us to expect least. A romantic, escaping from a drily intellectual theology, might easily be betrayed into valuing mere emotion and "religious experience" too highly: but in fact few nineteenth-century writers are more firmly catholic in relegating feeling to its proper place. (See Numbers 1, 27, 28, 37, 39, 351.) His whole philosophy of Nature

(Numbers 52, 67, 150, 151, 184, 185, 187, 188, 189, 285) with its resolute insistence on the concrete, owes little to the thought of an age which hovered between mechanism and idealism; he would obviously have been more at home with Professor Whitehead than with Herbert Spencer or T. H. Green. Number 285 seems to me particularly admirable. All romantics are vividly aware of mutability, but most of them are content to bewail it: for MacDonald this nostalgia is merely the starting point—he goes on and discovers what it is made for. His psychology also is worth noticing: he is quite as well aware as the moderns that the conscious self, the thing revealed by introspection, is a superficies. Hence the cellars and attics of the King's castle in *The Princess and the Goblins*, and the terror of his own house which falls upon Mr. Vane in *Lilith:* hence also his formidable critique (201) of our daily assumptions about the self. Perhaps most remarkable of all is the function—a low and primitive, yet often indispensable function—which he allows to Fear in the spiritual life (Numbers 3, 5, 6, 7, 137, 142, 143, 349). Reaction against early teachings might on this point have very easily driven him into a shallow liberalism. But it does not. He hopes, indeed, that all men will be saved; but that is because he hopes that all will repent. He knows (none better) that even omnipotence cannot save the unconverted. He never trifles with eternal impossibilities. He is as golden and genial as Traherne; but also as astringent as the *Imitation.*

So at least I have found him. In making this collection I was discharging a debt of justice. I have never concealed the fact that I regarded him as my master; indeed I fancy I have never written a book in which I did not quote from him. But it has not seemed to me that those who have received my books kindly take even now sufficient notice of the affiliation. Honesty drives me to emphasize it. And even if honesty did not—well, I am a don, and "source-hunting" (*Quellenforschung*) is perhaps in my marrow. It must be more than thirty years ago that I bought—almost unwillingly, for I had looked at the volume on that bookstall and rejected it on a dozen previous occasions—the Everyman edition of *Phantastes.* A few hours later I knew that I had crossed a great frontier. I had already been waist-deep in Romanticism; and likely enough, at any moment, to flounder into its darker and more evil forms, slithering down the steep descent that leads from the love of strangeness to that of eccentricity and thence to that of perversity. Now *Phantastes* was romantic enough in all conscience; but there was a difference. Nothing was at that time further from my thoughts than Christianity and I therefore had no notion what this difference really was. I was only aware that if this new world was strange, it was also homely and humble; that if this was a dream, it was a dream in which one at least felt strangely vigilant; that the whole book had about it a sort of cool, morning innocence, and also, quite unmistakably, a certain quality of Death, *good* Death. What it actually did to me was to convert, even to baptize (that was where the Death came in) my imagination. It did nothing to my intellect nor (at that time) to my conscience. Their turn came far later and with the help of many other books and men. But when the process was complete—by which, of course, I mean "when it had *really* begun"—I found that I was still with MacDonald and that he had accompanied me all the way and that I was now at last ready to hear from him much that he could not have told me at that first meeting. But in a sense, what he was now telling me was the very same that he had told me from the beginning. There was no question of getting through to the kernel and throwing away the shell: no question of a gilded pill. The pill was gold all through. The quality which had enchanted me in his imaginative works turned out to be the quality of the real universe, the divine, magical, terrifying, and ecstatic reality in which we all live. I should have been shocked in my teens if anyone had told me that what I learned to love in *Phantastes* was goodness. But now that I know, I see there was no deception. The deception is all the other way round—in that prosaic moralism which confines goodness to the region of Law and Duty, which never lets us feel in our face the sweet air blowing from "the land of righteousness," never reveals that elusive Form which if once seen must inevitably be desired with all but sensuous desire—the thing (in Sappho's phrase) "more gold than gold."

It is no part of my aim to produce a critical text of MacDonald. Apart from my unconscious errors in transcription, I have "tampered" in two ways. The whole difficulty of making extracts is to leave the sense perfectly clear while not retaining anything you do not want. In attempting to do so, I have sometimes interpolated a word (always enclosed in brackets) and sometimes altered the punctuation. I have also introduced a capital H for pronouns that refer to God, which the printer, in some of my originals, did not employ; not because I consider this typographical reverence of much importance, but because, in a language where pronouns are so easily confused as they are in English, it seems foolish to reject such an aid to clarity.

C. S. Lewis

GEORGE MACDONALD
AN ANTHOLOGY

[1]   *Dryness*

That man is perfect in faith who can come to God in the utter dearth of his feelings and desires, without a glow or an aspiration, with the weight of low thoughts, failures, neglects, and wandering forgetfulness, and say to Him, "Thou art my refuge."[1]

[2]   *Inexorable Love*

Nothing is inexorable but love. Love which will yield to prayer is imperfect and poor. Nor is it then the love that yields, but its alloy. . . . For love loves unto purity. Love has ever in view the absolute loveliness of that which it beholds. Where loveliness is incomplete, and

---

[1]The source of this quotation and of the subsequent quotations will be found in "Sources," which begins on page 175.

love cannot love its fill of loving, it spends itself to make more lovely, that it may love more; it strives for perfection, even that itself may be perfected—not in itself, but in the object.... Therefore all that is not beautiful in the beloved, all that comes between and is not of love's kind, must be destroyed. And our God is a consuming fire.

[3]   *Divine Burning*

He will shake heaven and earth, that only the unshakable may remain: he is a consuming fire, that only that which cannot be consumed may stand forth eternal. It is the nature of God, so terribly pure that it destroys all that is not pure as fire, which demands like purity in our worship. He will have purity. It is not that the fire will burn us if we do not worship thus; yea, will go on burning within us after all that is foreign to it has yielded to its force, no longer with pain and consuming, but as the highest consciousness of life, the presence of God.

[4] *The Beginning of Wisdom*

How should the Hebrews be other than terrified at that which was opposed to all they knew of themselves, beings judging it good to honor a golden calf? Such as they were, they did well to be afraid. . . . Fear is nobler than sensuality. Fear is better than no God, better than a god made with hands. . . . The worship of fear is true, although very low: and though not acceptable to God in itself, for only the worship of spirit and of truth is acceptable to Him, yet even in his sight it is precious. For He regards men not as they are merely, but as they shall be; not as they shall be merely, but as they are now growing, or capable of growing, toward that image after which He made them that they might grow to it. Therefore a thousand stages, each in itself all but value-less, are of inestimable worth as the necessary and connected gradations of an infinite progress. A condition which of declension would indicate a devil, may of growth indicate a saint.

[5]   *The Unawakened*

Can it be any comfort to them to be told that God loves them so that He will burn them clean? . . . They do not want to be clean, and they cannot bear to be tortured.

[6]   *Sinai*

And is not God ready to do unto them even as they fear, though with another feeling and a different end from any which they are capable of supposing? He is against sin: insofar as, and while, they and sin are one, He is against them—against their desires, their aims, their fears, and their hopes; and thus He is altogether and always *for them*. That thunder and lightning and tempest, that blackness torn with the sound of a trumpet, that visible horror billowed with the voice of words, was all but a faint image . . . of what God thinks and feels against vileness and selfishness, of the unrest of unassuageable repulsion with which He regards such conditions.

[7] *No*

When we say that God is Love, do we teach men that their fear of Him is groundless? No. As much as they fear will come upon them, possibly far more.... The wrath will consume what they *call* themselves; so that the selves God made shall appear.

[8] *The Law of Nature*

For that which cannot be shaken shall remain. That which is immortal in God shall remain in man. The death that is in them shall be consumed. It is the law of Nature—that is, the law of God—that all that is destructible shall be destroyed.

[9] *Escape Is Hopeless*

The man whose deeds are evil, fears the burning. But the burning will not come the less that he fears it or denies it. Escape is hopeless. For Love is inexorable. Our God is a consuming fire. He shall not come out till he has paid the uttermost farthing.

[10]   *The Word*

But herein is the Bible itself greatly wronged. It nowhere lays claim to be regarded as *the* Word, *the* Way, *the* Truth. The Bible leads us to Jesus, the inexhaustible, the ever unfolding Revelation of God. It is Christ "in whom are hid all the treasures of wisdom and knowledge," not the Bible, save as leading to Him.

[11]   *I Knew a Child*

I knew a child who believed she had committed the sin against the Holy Ghost, because she had, in her toilette, made an improper use of a pin. Dare not to rebuke me for adducing the diseased fancy of a child in a weighty matter of theology. "Despise not one of these little ones." Would the theologians were as near the truth in such matters as the children. *Diseased fancy!* The child knew, *and was conscious that she knew,* that she was doing wrong because she had been forbidden. There was rational ground for her fear. . . . *He* would not have told her she was silly, and "never to mind." Child as she was, might He not have said to her, "I do not condemn thee: and go and sin no more"?

[12]   *Spiritual Murder*

It may be an infinitely less evil to murder a man than to refuse to forgive him. The former may be the act of a moment of passion: the latter is the heart's choice. It is spiritual murder, the worst, to hate, to brood over the feeling that excludes, that, in our microcosm, kills the image, the idea of the hated.

[13]   *Impossibilities*

No man who will not forgive his neighbor, can believe that God is willing, yea wanting, to forgive *him*. . . . If God said, "I forgive you" to a man who hated his brother, and if (as impossible) that voice of forgiveness should reach the man, what would it mean to him? How much would the man interpret it? Would it not mean to him "You may go on hating. I do not mind it. You have had great provocation and are justified in your hate"? No doubt God takes what wrong there is, and what provocation there is, into the account: but the more provocation, the more excuse that can be urged for the hate, the more reason, if possible, that the hater should be delivered from the hell of his hate. . . . The man would think, not that God loved the sinner, but that he forgave the sin, which God never does [i.e., What is usually called "forgiving the sin" means forgiving the sinner and destroying the sin]. *Every* sin meets with its due fate—inexorable expulsion from the paradise of God's Humanity. He loves the sinner so much that He cannot forgive him in any other way than by banishing from his bosom the demon that possesses him.

[14] *Truth Is Truth*

Truth is truth, whether from the lips of Jesus or Balaam.

[15] *The White Stone*
(Revelations 2:17)

The giving of the white stone with the new name is the communication of what God thinks about the man to the man. It is the divine judgment, the solemn holy doom of the righteous man, the "Come, thou blessed," spoken to the individual.... The true name is one which expresses the character, the nature, the *meaning* of the person who bears it. It is the man's own symbol—his soul's picture, in a word—the sign which belongs to him and to no one else. Who can give a man this, his own name? God alone. For no one but God sees what the man is.... It is only when the man has become his name that God gives him the stone with the name upon it, for then first can he understand what his name signifies. It is the blossom, the perfection, the completeness, that determines the name: and God foresees that from the first because He made it so: but the tree of the soul, before its blossom comes, cannot understand what blossom it is to bear and could not know what the word meant, which, in representing its own unarrived completeness, named itself. Such a name cannot be given until the man *is* the name. God's name for a man must be the expression of His own idea of the man, that being whom He had in His thought when he began to make the child, and whom He kept in His thought through the long process of creation that went to realize the idea. To tell the name is to seal the success—to say "In thee also I am well pleased."

[16]   *Personality*

The name is one "which no man knoweth saving he that receiveth it." Not only then has each man his individual relation to God, but each man has his peculiar relation to God. He is to God a peculiar being, made after his own fashion, and that of no one else. Hence he can worship God as no man else can worship Him.

[17]   *The Secret in Man*

For each, God has a different response. With every man He has a secret—the secret of a new name. In every man there is a loneliness, an inner chamber of peculiar life into which God only can enter. I say not it is *the innermost chamber.*

[18]   *The Secrets in God*

There is a chamber also (O God, humble and accept my speech)—a chamber in God Himself, into which none can enter but the one, the individual, the peculiar man—out of which chamber that man has to bring revelation and strength for his brethren. This is that for which he was made—to reveal the secret things of the Father.

[19]   *No Massing*

There is no massing of men with God. When he speaks of gathered men, it is as a spiritual *body*, not as a *mass*.

[20]   *No Comparing*

Here there is no room for ambition. Ambition is the desire to be above one's neighbor; and here there is no possibility of comparison with one's neighbor: no one knows what the white stone contains except the man who receives it.... Relative worth is not only unknown—to the children of the Kingdom it is unknowable.

[21] *The End*

"God has cared to make me for Himself," says the victor with the white stone, "And has called me that which I like best."

[22] *Moth and Rust*

What is with the treasure must fare as the treasure.... The heart which haunts the treasure house where the moth and rust corrupt, will be exposed to the same ravages as the treasure.... Many a man, many a woman, fair and flourishing to see, is going about with a rusty moth-eaten heart within that form of strength or beauty. "But this is only a figure." True. But is the reality intended, less or more than the figure?

[23] *Caverns and Films*

If God sees that heart corroded with the rust of cares, riddled into caverns and films by the worms of ambition and greed, then your heart is as God sees it, for

God sees things as they are. And one day you will be compelled to see, nay, to *feel* your heart as God sees it.

[24]   *Various Kinds of Moth*

Nor does the lesson apply to those only who worship Mammon.... It applies to those equally who in any way worship the transitory; who seek the praise of men more than the praise of God; who would make a show in the world by wealth, by taste, by intellect, by power, by art, by genius of any kind, and so would gather golden opinions to be treasured in a storehouse of earth. Nor to such only, but surely to those as well whose pleasures are of a more evidently transitory nature still, such as the pleasures of the senses in every direction—whether lawfully indulged, if the joy of being is centered in them—do these words bear terrible warning. For the hurt lies not in this—that these pleasures are false like the deceptions of magic, for such they are not; ... nor yet in this—that they pass away and leave a fierce disappointment behind; that is only so much the better; but the hurt lies in this—that the immortal, the infinite, created in the image of the everlasting God, is housed with the fading and the corrupting, and clings to them as its good—clings to them till it is infected and interpenetrated with their proper diseases, which assume in it a form more terrible in proportion to the superiority of its kind.

[25]   *Holy Scriptures*

This story may not be just as the Lord told it, and yet may contain in its mirror as much of the truth as we are able to receive, and as will afford us scope for a life's discovery. The modifying influence of the human channels may be essential to God's revealing mode.

[26]   *Command That These Stones Be Made Bread*

The Father said, That is a stone. The Son would not say, That is a loaf. No one creative *Fiat* shall contradict another. The Father and the Son are of one mind. The Lord could hunger, could starve, but would not change into another thing what His Father had made one thing. There was no such change in the feeding of the multitudes. The fish and the bread were fish and bread before. . . . There was in these miracles, and I think in all, only a hastening of appearances: the doing of that in a day, which may ordinarily take a thousand years, for with God time is not what it is with us. He makes it. . . . Nor does it render the process one whit more miraculous. Indeed, the wonder of the growing corn is to me greater than the wonder of feeding the thousands. It is easier to understand the creative power going forth at once—immediately—than through the countless, the lovely, the seemingly forsaken wonders of the corn-field.

[27]   *Religious Feeling*

In the higher aspect of this first temptation, arising from the fact that a man cannot feel the things he believes except under certain conditions of physical well-being dependent upon food, the answer is the same: A man does not live by his feelings any more than by bread.

[28] *Dryness*

And when he can no longer *feel* the truth, he shall not therefore die. He lives because God is true; and he is able to know that he lives because he knows, having once understood the word that God is truth. He believes in the God of former vision, lives by that word therefore, when all is dark and there is no vision.

[29] *Presumption*

"If ye have faith and doubt not, if ye shall say unto this mountain, Be thou removed and cast into the sea, it shall be done." Good people . . . have been tempted to tempt the Lord their God upon the strength of this say- ing. . . . Happily for such, the assurance to which they would give the name of faith generally fails them in time. Faith is that which, knowing the Lord's will, goes and does it; or, not knowing it, stands and waits. . . . But to put God to the question in any other way than by saying, "What wilt thou have me to do?" is an attempt to compel God to declare Himself, or to hasten His work. . . . The man is therein dissociating himself from God so far that, instead of acting by the divine will from within, he acts in God's face, as it were, to see what He will do. Man's first business is, "What does God want me to do?", not "What will God do if I do so and so?"

[30]   *The Knowledge of God*

To say *Thou art God,* without knowing what the *Thou* means—of what use is it? God is a name only, except we know *God.*

[31]   *The Passion*

It is with the holiest fear that we should approach the terrible fact of the sufferings of Our Lord. Let no one think that these were less because He was more. The more delicate the nature, the more alive to all that is lovely and true, lawful and right, the more does it feel the antagonism of pain, the inroad of death upon life; the more dreadful is that breach of the harmony of things whose sound is torture.

[32] *Eli, Eli*

He could not see, could not feel Him near; and yet it is "My God" that He cries. Thus the Will of Jesus, in the very moment when His faith seems about to yield is finally triumphant. It has no *feeling* now to support it, no beatific vision to absorb it. It stands naked in His soul and tortured, as He stood naked and scourged before Pilate. Pure and simple and surrounded by fire, it declares for God.

[33] *The Same*

Without this last trial of all, the temptations of our Master had not been so full as the human cup could hold; there would have been one region through which we had to pass wherein we might call aloud upon our Captain-Brother, and there would be no voice or hearing: He had avoided the fatal spot!

[34]   *Vicarious Desolation*

This is the Faith of the Son of God. God withdrew, as it were, that the perfect Will of the Son might arise and go forth to find the Will of the Father. It is possible that even then He thought of the lost sheep who could not believe that God was their Father; and for them, too, in all their loss and blindness and unlove, cried, saying the word they might say, knowing for them that *God* means *Father* and more.

[35]   *Creeping Christians*

We are and remain such creeping Christians, because we look at ourselves and not at Christ; because we gaze at the marks of our own soiled feet, and the trail of our own defiled garments. . . . Each, putting his foot in the footprint of the Master, and so defacing it, turns to examine how far his neighbor's footprint corresponds with that which he still calls the Master's, although it is but his own. Or, having committed a petty fault, I mean a fault such as only a petty creature could commit, we mourn over the defilement to ourselves, and the shame of it before our friends, children, or servants, instead of hastening to make the due confession and amends to our fellow, and then, forgetting our own paltry self with its well-earned disgrace, lift up our eyes to the glory which alone will quicken the true man in us, and kill the peddling creature we so wrongly call our *self*.

[36] *Dryness*

So long as we have nothing to say to God, nothing to do with Him, save in the sunshine of the mind when we feel Him near us, we are poor creatures, willed upon, not willing. . . . And how in such a condition do we generally act? Do we sit mourning over the loss of feeling? Or worse, make frantic efforts to rouse them?

[37] *The Use of Dryness*

God does not, by the instant gift of His Spirit, make us always feel right, desire good, love purity, aspire after Him and His Will. Therefore either He will not, or He cannot. If He will not, it must be because it would not be well to do so. If He cannot, then He would not if He could; else a better condition than God's is conceivable to the mind of God. . . . The truth is this: He wants to make us in His own image, *choosing* the good, *refusing* the evil. How should He effect this if He were *always* moving us from within, as He does at divine intervals, toward the beauty of holiness? . . . For God made our individuality as well as, and a greater marvel than, our dependence; made our *apartness* from Himself, that freedom should bind us divinely dearer to Himself, with a new and inscrutable marvel of love; for the Godhead is still at the root, is the making root of our individuality, and the freer the man, the stronger the bond that binds him to Him who made his freedom.

[38] *The Highest Condition of the Human Will*

The highest condition of the human will is in sight. . . . I say not the highest condition of the Human Being; that surely lies in the Beatific Vision, in the sight of God. But the highest condition of the Human Will, as distinct, not as separated from God, is when, not seeing God, not seeming to itself to grasp Him at all, it yet holds Him fast.

[39]   *Troubled Soul*

Troubled soul, thou are not bound to feel but thou art bound to arise. God loves thee whether thou feelest or not. Thou canst not love when thou wilt, but thou art bound to fight the hatred in thee to the last. Try not to feel good when thou art not good, but cry to Him who is good. He changes not because thou changest. Nay, He has an especial tenderness of love toward thee for that thou art in the dark and hast no light, and His heart is glad when thou doest arise and say, "I will go to my Father." . . . Fold the arms of thy faith, and wait in the quietness until light goes up in thy darkness. For the arms of thy Faith I say, but not of thy Action: bethink thee of something that thou oughtest to do, and go to do it, if it be but the sweeping of a room, or the preparing of a meal, or a visit to a friend. Heed not thy feeling: Do thy work.

[40]   *Dangerous Moment*

Am I going to do a good deed? Then, of all times—Father into thy hands: lest the enemy should have me now.

[41] *It Is Finished*

. . . when the agony of death was over, when the storm of the world died away behind His retiring spirit, and He entered the regions where there is only life, and therefore all that is not music is silence. . . .

[42] *Members of One Another*

We shall never be able, I say, to rest in the bosom of the Father, till the fatherhood is fully revealed to us in the love of the brothers. For He cannot be our Father, save as He is their Father; and if we do not see Him and feel Him as their Father, we cannot know Him as ours.

[43] *Originality*

Our Lord never thought of being original.

[44] *The Moral Law*

Of what use then is the Law? To lead us to Christ, the Truth—to waken in our minds a sense of what our deepest nature, the presence, namely, of God *in* us, requires of us—to let us know, in part by failure, that the purest efforts of will of which we are capable cannot lift us up even to the abstaining from wrong to our neighbor.

[45] *The Same*

In order to fulfill the commonest law . . . we must rise into a loftier region altogether, a region that is above law, because it is spirit and life and makes the law.

[46] *Upward toward the Center*

"But how," says a man, who is willing to recognize the universal neighborhood, but finds himself unable to fulfill the bare law toward the woman even whom he loves best—"How am I then to rise into that higher region, that empyrean of love?" And, beginning straightaway to try to love his neighbor, he finds that the empyrean of which he spoke is no more to be reached in itself than the law was to be reached in itself. As he cannot keep the law without first rising into the love of his neighbor, so he cannot love his neighbor without first rising higher still. The whole system of the universe works upon this law—the driving of things upward toward the center. The man who will love his neighbor can do so by no immediately operative exercise of the will. It is the man fulfilled of God from whom he came and by whom he is, who alone can as himself love his neighbor who came from God too and is by God too. The mystery of individuality and consequent relation is deep as the beginnings of humanity, and the questions thence arising can be solved only by him who has, practically at least, solved the holy necessities resulting from his origin. In God alone can man meet man. In Him alone the converging lines of existence touch and cross not. When the mind of Christ, the life of the Head, courses through that atom which the man is of the slowly revivifying body, when he is alive too, then the love of the brothers is there as conscious life. . . . It *is* possible to love our neighbor as ourselves. Our Lord *never* spoke hyperbolically.

[47]   *No One Loves Because He Sees Why*

Where a man does not love, the not-loving must seem rational. For no one loves because he sees why, but because he loves. No human reason can be given for the highest necessity of divinely created existence. For reasons are always from above downward.

[48]   *My Neighbor*

A man must not choose his neighbor: he must take the neighbor that God sends him. . . . The neighbor is just the man who is next to you at the moment, the man with whom any business has brought you into contact.

[49]   *The Same*

The love of our neighbor is the only door out of the dungeon of self, where we mope and mow, striking sparks, and rubbing phosphorescences out of the walls, and blowing our own breath in our own nostrils, instead of issuing to the fair sunlight of God, the sweet winds of the universe.

[50]   *What Cannot Be Loved*

But how can we love a man or a woman who ... is mean, unlovely, carping, uncertain, self-righteous, self-seeking, and self-admiring?—who can even sneer, the most inhuman of human faults, far worse in its essence than mere murder? These things cannot be loved. The best man hates them most; the worst man cannot love them. But are these the man?... Lies there not within the man and the woman a divine element of brotherhood, of sisterhood, a something lovely and lovable—slowly fading, it may be—dying away under the fierce heat of vile passions, or the yet more fearful cold of sepulchral selfishness, but there?... It is the very presence of this fading humanity that makes it possible for us to hate. If it were an animal only, and not a man or a woman, that did us hurt, we should not hate: we should only kill.

[51]   *Love and Justice*

Man is not made for justice from his fellow, but for love, which is greater than justice, and by including supersedes justice. *Mere* justice is an impossibility, a fiction of analysis.... Justice to be justice must be much more than justice. Love is the law of our condition, without which we can no more render justice than a man can keep a straight line, walking in the dark.

[52]   *The Body*

It is by the body that we come into contact with Nature, with our fellowmen, with all their revelations to us. It is through the body that we receive all the lessons of passion, of suffering, of love, of beauty, of science. It is through the body that we are both trained outward from ourselves, and driven inward into our deepest selves to find God. There is glory and might in this vital evanescence, this slow glacierlike flow of clothing and revealing matter, this ever uptossed rainbow of tangible humanity. It is no less of God's making than the spirit that is clothed therein.

[53] *Goodness*

The Father was all in all to the Son, and the Son no more thought of His own goodness than an honest man thinks of his honesty. When the good man sees goodness, he thinks of his own evil: Jesus had no evil to think of, but neither does He think of His goodness: He delights in His Father's. "Why callest thou Me good?"

[54] *Christ's Disregards*

The Lord cared neither for isolated truth nor for orphaned deed. It was truth in the inward parts, it was the good heart, the mother of good deeds, He cherished. . . . It was good men He cared about, not notions of good things, or even good actions, save as the outcome of life, save as the bodies in which the primary live actions of love and will in the soul took shape and came forth.

[55] *Easy to Please and Hard to Satisfy*

That no keeping but a perfect one will *satisfy* God, I hold with all my heart and strength; but that there is none else He cares for, is one of the lies of the enemy. What father is not pleased with the first tottering attempt of his little one to walk? What father would be satisfied with anything but the manly step of the full-grown son?

[56] *The Moral Law*

The immediate end of the commandments never was that men should succeed in obeying them, but that, finding they could not do that which yet must be done, finding the more they tried the more was required of them, they should be driven to the source of life and law—of their life and His law—to seek from Him such reinforcement of life as should make the fulfillment of the law as possible, yea, as natural, as necessary.

[57]   *Bondage*

A man is in bondage to whatever he cannot part with that is less than himself.

[58]   *The Rich Young Man*
(Matthew 19:16–22)

It was time . . . that he should refuse, that he should know what manner of spirit he was of, and meet the confusions of soul, the sad searchings of heart that must follow. A time comes to every man when he must obey, or make such refusal—*and know it.* . . . The time will come, God only knows its hour, when he will see the nature of his deed, *with the knowledge that he was dimly seeing it so even when he did it:* the alternative had been put before him.

[59]   *Law and Spirit*

The commandments can never be kept while there is a strife to keep them: the man is overwhelmed in the weight of their broken pieces. It needs a clean heart to have pure hands, all the power of a live soul to keep the law—a power of life, not of struggle; the strength of love, not the effort of duty.

[60] *Our Nonage*

The number of fools not yet acknowledging the first condition of manhood nowise alters the fact that he who *has* begun to recognize duty and acknowledge the facts of his being, is but a tottering child on the path of life. He is on the path: he is as wise as at the time he can be; the Father's arms are stretched out to receive him; but he is not therefore a wonderful being; not therefore a model of wisdom; not at all the admirable creature his largely remaining folly would, in his worst moments (that is, when he feels best) persuade him to think himself; he is just one of God's poor creatures.

[61]   *Knowledge*

Had he done as the Master told him, he would soon have come to understand. Obedience is the opener of eyes.

[62]   *Living Forever*

The poor idea of living forever, all that commonplace minds grasp at for eternal life—(is) its mere concomitant shadow, in itself not worth thinking about. When a man is . . . one with God, what should he do but live forever?

[63]   *Be Ye Perfect*

"I cannot be perfect; it is hopeless; and He does not expect it."—It would be more honest if he said, "I do not want to be perfect: I am content to be saved." Such as he do not care for being perfect as their Father in heaven is perfect, but for being what they called *saved*.

[64]   *Carrion Comfort*

Or are you so well satisfied with what you are, that you have never sought eternal life, never hungered and thirsted after the righteousness of God, the perfection of your being? If this latter be your condition, then be comforted; the Master does not require of you to sell what you have and give to the poor. *You* follow Him! *You* go with Him to preach good tidings!—you who care not for righteousness! You are not one whose company is desirable to the Master. Be comforted, I say: He does not want you; He will not ask you to open your purse for Him; you may give or withhold: it is nothing to Him. . . . *Go and keep the commandments.* It is not come to your money yet. The commandments are enough for you. You are not yet a child in the kingdom. You do not care for the arms of your Father; you value only the shelter of His roof. As to your money, let the commandments direct you how to use it. It is in you but pitiable presumption to wonder whether it is required of you to sell all that you have . . . for the Young Man to have sold all and followed Him would have been to accept God's patent of peerage: to you it is not offered.

[65]   *The Same*

Does this comfort you? Then alas for you! ... Your relief is to know that the Lord has no need of you— does not require you to part with your money, does not offer you Himself instead. You do not indeed sell Him for thirty pieces of silver, but you are glad not to buy Him with all that you have.

[66]   *How Hard?*

This life, this Kingdom of God, this simplicity of absolute existence, is hard to enter. How hard? As hard as the Master of salvation could find words to express the hardness.

[67]   *Things*

The man who for consciousness of well-being depends upon anything but life, the life essential, is a slave; he hangs on what is less than himself. ... *Things* are given us—this body, first of things—that through them we may be trained both to independence and true possession of them. We must possess them; they must not possess us. Their use is to mediate—as shapes and manifestations in lower kind of the things that are unseen, that is, in themselves unseeable, the things that belong, not to the world of speech but the world of silence, not to the world of showing, but the world of being, the world that cannot be shaken, and must remain. These things unseen take the form in the things of time and space—not that they may exist, for they exist in and from eternal Godhead, but that their being may be known to those in training for the eternal; these things unseen the sons and daughters of God must possess. But instead of reaching out after them, they grasp at their forms, regard the things seen as the things to be possessed, fall in love with the bodies instead of the souls of them.

[68] *Possession*

He who has God, has all things, after the fashion in which He who made them has them.

[69]   *The Torment of Death*

It is imperative on us to get rid of the tyranny of things. See how imperative: let the young man cling with every fiber to his wealth, what God can do He will do; His child shall not be left in the Hell of possession. Comes the angel of death—and where are the things that haunted the poor soul with such manifold hindrance and obstruction? . . . Is the man so freed from the dominion of things? Does Death so serve him—so ransom him? . . . Not so; for then first, I presume, does the man of things become aware of their tyranny. When a man begins to abstain, then first he recognizes the strength of his passion: it may be, when a man has not a thing left, he will begin to know what a necessity he had made of things.

[70]   *The Utility of Death*

Wherein then lies the service of Death? . . . In this: it is not the fetters that gall, but the fetters that soothe, which eat into the soul. In this way is the loss of things . . . a motioning, hardly toward, yet in favor of, deliverance. It may seem to a man the first of his slavery when it is in truth the beginning of his freedom. Never soul was set free without being made to feel its slavery.

[71]   *Not the Rich Only*

But it is not the rich man only who is under the dominion of things; they too are slaves who, having no money, are unhappy from the lack of it.

[72]   *Fearful Thinking*

Because we easily imagine ourselves in want, we imagine God ready to forsake us.

[73]   *Miracles*

The miracles of Jesus were the ordinary works of His Father, wrought small and swift that we might take them in.

[74]   *The Sacred Present*

The next hour, the next moment, is as much beyond our grasp and as much in God's care, as that a hundred years away. Care for the next minute is just as foolish as care for the morrow, or for a day in the next thousand years—in neither can we do anything, in both God is doing everything. Those claims only of the morrow which have to be prepared today are of the duty of today: the moment which coincides with work to be done, is the moment to be minded; the next is nowhere till God has made it.

[75]   *Forethought*

If a man forget a thing, God will see to that: man is not Lord of his memory or his intellect. But man is lord of his will, his action; and is then verily to blame when, remembering a duty, he does not do it, but puts it off, and *so* forgets it. If a man lay himself out to do the immediate duty of the moment, wonderfully little forethought, I suspect, will be found needful. That forethought only is right which has to determine duty, and pass into action. To the foundation of yesterday's work well done, the work of the morrow will be sure to fit. Work done is of more consequence for the future than the foresight of an archangel.

[76]   *Not the Rich Only*

If it be *things* that slay you, what matter whether things you have, or things you have not?

[77]   *Care*

Tomorrow makes today's whole head sick, its whole heart faint. When we should be still, sleeping or dreaming, we are fretting about an hour that lies a half sun's journey away! Not so doest thou, Lord; thou doest the work of thy Father!

[78]   *The Sacred Present*

The care that is filling your mind at this moment, or but waiting till you lay the book aside to leap upon you—

that need which is no need, is a demon sucking at the spring of your life. "No; mine is a reasonable care—an unavoidable care, indeed." Is it something you have to do this very moment? "No." Then you are allowing it to usurp the place of something that is required of you this moment. "There is nothing required of me at this moment." Nay but there is—the greatest thing that can be required of man. "Pray, what is it?" Trust in the living God. . . . "I do trust Him in spiritual matters." Everything is an affair of the spirit.

[79] *Heaven*

For the only air of the soul, in which it can breathe and live, is the present God and the spirits of the just: that is our heaven, our home, our all-right place. . . . We shall be God's children on the little hills and in the fields of that heaven, not one desiring to be before another any more than to cast that other out; for ambition and hatred will then be seen to be one and the same spirit.

[80] *Shaky Foundations*

The things readiest to be done, those which lie, not at the door but on the very table, of a man's mind, are not merely in general the most neglected, but even by the thoughtful man, the oftenest let alone, the oftenest postponed. . . . Truth is one, and he who does the truth in the small thing is of the truth; he who will do it only in a great thing, who postpones the small thing near him to the great farther from him, is not of the truth.

[81] *Fussing*

We, too, dull our understandings with trifles, fill the heavenly spaces with phantoms, waste the heavenly time with hurry. When I trouble myself over a trifle, even a trifle confessed—the loss of some little article, say—spurring my memory, and hunting the house, not from immediate need, but from dislike of loss; when a book has been borrowed of me and not returned, and I have forgotten the borrower, and fret over the missing volume . . . is it not time I lost a few things when I care for them so unreasonably? This losing of things is of the mercy of God: it comes to teach us to let them go.

Or have I forgotten a thought that came to me, which seemed of the truth? . . . I keep trying and trying to call it back, feeling a poor man till that thought be recovered to be far more lost, perhaps, in a notebook, into which I shall never look again to find it! I forgot that it is live things God cares about.

[82]   *Housekeeping*

I appeal especially to all who keep house concerning the size of troubles that suffices to hide word and face of God.

[83]   *Cares*

With every haunting trouble then, great or small, the loss of thousands or the lack of a shilling, go to God. . . . If your trouble is such that you cannot appeal to Him, the more need you should appeal to him!

[84]   *God at the Door*

Nor will God force any door to enter in. He may send a tempest about the house; the wind of His admonishment may burst doors and windows, yea, shake the house to its foundations; but not then, not so, will He enter. The door must be opened by the willing hand, ere the foot of Love will cross the threshold. He watches to see the door move from within. Every tempest is but an assault in the siege of Love. The terror of God is but the other side of His love; it is love outside, that would be inside—love that knows the house is no house, only a place, until it enter.

[85]   *Difficulties*

Everything difficult indicates something more than our theory of life yet embraces, checks some tendency to abandon the straight path, leaving open only the way ahead. But there is a reality of being in which all things are easy and plain—oneness, that is, with the Lord of Life; to pray for this is the first thing; and to the point of this prayer every difficulty hedges and directs us.

[86] *Vain Vigilance*

Do those who say, "Lo here or lo there are the signs of His coming," think to be too keen for Him, and spy His approach? When he tells them to watch lest He find them neglecting their work, they state this way and that, and watch lest He should succeed in coming like a thief! . . . Obedience is the one key of life.

[87] *Incompleteness*

He that is made in the image of God must know Him or be desolate. . . . Witness the dissatisfaction, yea, desolation of my soul—wretched, alone, unfinished, without Him. It cannot act from itself, save in God; acting from what seems itself without God, is no action at all, it is a mere yielding to impulse. All within is disorder and spasm. There is a cry behind me, and a voice before; instincts of betterment tell me I must rise above my present self—perhaps even above all my possible self: I see not how to obey, how to carry them out! I am shut up in a world of consciousness, an unknown I in an unknown world: surely this world of my unwilled, unchosen, compelled existence, cannot be shut out from Him, cannot be unknown to Him, cannot be impenetrable, impermeable, unpresent to Him from whom I am?

[88] *Prayer*

Shall I not tell Him my troubles—how He, even He, has troubled me by making me?—how unfit I am to be that which I am?—that my being is not to me a good thing yet?—that I need a law that shall account to me for it in righteousness—reveal to me how I am to make it a good—how I am to *be* a good and not an evil?

[89] *Knowledge That Would Be Useless*

Why should the question admit of doubt? We know that the wind blows; why should we not know that God answers prayer? I reply, What if God does not care to have you know it at secondhand? What if there would be no good in that? There is some testimony on record, and perhaps there might be much were it not that, having to do with things so immediately personal, and generally so delicate, answers to prayer would naturally not often be talked about; but no testimony concerning the thing can well be conclusive; for, like a reported miracle, there is always some way to daff it; and besides, the conviction to be got that way is of little value: it avails nothing to know the thing by the best of evidence.

[90]   *Prayer*

Reader, if you are in any trouble, try whether God will not help you: if you are in no need, why should you ask questions about prayer? True, he knows little of himself who does not know that he is wretched, and miserable, and poor, and blind, and naked; but until he begins at least to suspect a need, how can he pray?

[91]   *Why Should It Be Necessary?*

"But if God is so good as you represent Him, and if He knows all that we need, and better far than we do ourselves, why should it be necessary to ask Him for anything?" I answer, What if He knows Prayer to be the thing we need first and most? What if the main object in God's idea of prayer be the supplying of our great, our endless need—the need of Himself? ... Hunger may drive the runaway child home, and he may or may not be fed at once, but he needs his mother more than his dinner. Communion with God is the one need of the soul beyond all other need: prayer is the beginning of that communion, and some need is the motive of that prayer. ... So begins a communion, a taking with God, a coming-to-one with Him, which is the sole end of prayer, yea, of existence itself in its infinite phases. We must ask that we may receive: but that we should receive what we ask in respect of our lower needs, is not God's end in making us pray, for He could give us everything without that: to bring His child to his knee, God withholds that man may ask.

[92]   *The Conditions of a Good Gift*

For the real good of every gift is essential first, that the giver be in the gift—as God always is, for He is love—and next, that the receiver know and receive the giver in the gift. Every gift of God is but a harbinger of His greatest and only sufficing gift—that of Himself. No gift unrecognized as coming from God is at its own best: therefore many things that God would gladly give us, things even that we need because we are, must wait until we ask for them, that we may know whence they come: when in all gifts we find Him, then in Him we shall find all things.

[93] *False Spirituality*

Sometimes to one praying will come the feeling ... "Were it not better to abstain? If this thing be good, will He not give it me? Would He not be better pleased if I left it altogether to Him?" It comes, I think, of a lack of faith and childlikeness ... it may even come of ambition after spiritual distinction.

[94] *Small Prayers*

In every request, heart and soul and mind ought to supply the low accompaniment, "Thy will be done"; but the making of any request brings us near to Him. ...

Anything large enough for a wish to light upon, is large enough to hang a prayer upon: the thought of Him to whom that prayer goes will purify and correct the desire.

[95]   *Riches and Need*

There could be no riches but for need. God Himself is made rich by man's necessity. By that He is rich to give; through that we are rich by receiving.

[96]   *Providence*

"How should any design of the All-wise be altered in response to prayer of ours? How are we to believe such a thing?" By reflecting that He is the All-wise, who sees before Him, and will not block His path. . . . Does God care for suns and planets and satellites, for divine mathematics and ordered harmonies, more than for His children? I venture to say He cares more for oxen than for those. He lays no plans irrespective of His children;

and, His design being that they shall be free, active, live things, He sees that space shall be kept for them.

[97]   *Divine Freedom*

What stupidity of perfection would that be which left no margin about God's work, no room for change of plan upon change of fact—yea, even the mighty change that ... now at length His child is praying! ... I may move my arm as I please: shall God be unable so to move His?

[98]   *Providence*

If His machine interfered with His answering the prayer of a single child, He would sweep it from Him—not to bring back chaos but to make room for His child. ... We must remember that God is not occupied with a grand toy of worlds and suns and planets, of attractions and repulsions, of agglomerations and crystallizations, of forces and waves; that these but constitute a portion of His workshops and tools for the bringing out of righteous men and women to fill His house of love withal.

[99]   *The Miracles of Our Lord*

In all His miracles Jesus did only in miniature what His Father does ever in the great. Poor, indeed, was the making of the wine in the . . . pots of stone, compared with its making in the lovely growth of the vine with its clusters of swelling grapes—the live roots gathering from the earth the water that had to be borne in pitchers and poured into the great vases; but it is precious as the interpreter of the same, even in its being the outcome of Our Lord's sympathy with ordinary human rejoicing.

[100]   *They Have No Wine*
         (John 2:3)

At the prayer of His mother, He made room in His plans for the thing she desired. It was not His wish then to work a miracle, but if His mother wished it, He would. He did for His mother what for His own part He would rather have left alone. Not always did He do as His mother would have Him; but this was a case in which He could do so, for it would interfere nowise with the will of His Father. . . . The Son, then, could change His intent and spoil nothing: so, I say, can the Father; for the Son does nothing but what He sees the Father do.

[101] *Intercessory Prayer*

And why should the good of anyone depend on the prayer of another? I can only answer with the return question, "Why should my love be powerless to help another?"

[102] *The Eternal Revolt*

There is endless room for rebellion against ourselves.

[103]   *They Say It Does Them Good*

There are those even who, not believing in any ear to
hear, any heart to answer, will yet pray. They say it does
them good; they pray to nothing at all, but they get
spiritual benefit. I will not contradict their testimony.
So needful is prayer to the soul that the mere attitude of
it may encourage a good mood. Verily to pray to that
which is not, is in logic a folly: yet the good that, they
say, comes of it, may rebuke the worse folly of their
unbelief, for it indicates that prayer is natural, and how
could it be natural if inconsistent with the very mode of
our being?

[104]   *Perfected Prayer*

And there is a communion with God that asks for
nothing, yet asks for everything. . . . He who seeks the
Father more than anything He can give, is likely to
have what he asks, for he is not likely to ask amiss.

[105]   *Corrective Granting*

Even such as ask amiss may sometimes have their prayers answered. The Father will never give the child a stone that asks for bread; but I am not sure that He will never give the child a stone that asks for a stone. If the Father says, "My child, that is a stone; it is no bread," and the child answer, "I am sure it is bread; I want it," may it not be well that he should try his "bread"?

[106]   *Why We Must Wait*

Perhaps, indeed, the better the gift we pray for, the more time is necessary for its arrival. To give us the spiritual gift we desire, God may have to begin far back in our spirit, in regions unknown to us, and do much work that we can be aware of only in the results; for our consciousness is to the extent of our being but as the flame of the volcano to the world-gulf whence it issues; in the gulf of our unknown being God works behind our consciousness. With His holy influence, with His own presence (the one thing for which most earnestly we cry) He may be approaching our consciousness from behind, coming forward through regions of our darkness into our light, long before we begin to be aware that He is answering our request—has answered it, and is visiting His child.

[107]   *God's Vengeance*

"Vengeance is mine," He says: with a right understanding of it, we might as well pray for God's vengeance as for His forgiveness; that vengeance is, to destroy the sin—to make the sinner abjure and hate it; nor is there any satisfaction in a vengeance that seeks or effects less. The man himself must turn against himself, and so be for himself. If nothing else will do, then hellfire; if less will do, whatever brings repentance and self-repudiation, is God's repayment. Friends, if any prayers are offered against us; if the vengeance of God be cried out for, because of some wrong you or I have done, God grant us His vengeance! Let us not think that we shall get off!

[108] *The Way of Understanding*

He who does that which he sees, shall understand; he who is set upon understanding rather than doing, shall go on stumbling and mistaking and speaking foolishness. . . . It is he that runneth that shall read, and no other. It is not intended by the Speaker of the Parables that any other should know intellectually what, known but intellectually, would be for his injury—what, knowing intellectually, he would imagine he had grasped, perhaps even appropriated. When the pilgrim of the truth comes on his journey to the region of the parable, he finds its interpretation. It is not a fruit or a jewel to be stored, but a well springing by the wayside.

[109] *Penal Blindness*

Those who by insincerity and falsehood close their deeper eyes, shall not be capable of using in the matter the more superficial eyes of their understanding. . . . This will help to remove the difficulty that the parables are plainly for the teaching of the truth, and yet the Lord speaks of them as for the concealing of it. They are for the understanding of that man only who is practical—who does the thing he knows, who seeks to understand vitally. They reveal to the live conscience, otherwise not to the keenest intellect.

[110] *The Same*

The former are content to have the light cast upon their way: the latter will have it in their eyes and cannot; if they had, it would blind them. For them to know more would be their worse condemnation. They are not fit to know more, more shall not be given them yet. . . . "You choose the dark; you shall stay in the dark till the terrors that dwell in the dark affray you, and cause you to cry out." God puts a seal upon the will of man; that seal is either His great punishment or His mighty favor: "Ye love the darkness, abide in the darkness": "O woman great is thy faith: be it done unto thee even as thou wilt!"

[111] *Agree with the Adversary Quickly*

Arrange what claim lies against you; compulsion waits behind it. Do at once what you must do one day. As there is no escape from payment, escape at least the prison that will enforce it. Do not drive justice to extremities. Duty is imperative; it must be done. It is useless to think to escape the eternal law of things: yield of yourself, nor compel God to compel you.

[112] *The Inexorable*

No, there is no escape. There is no heaven with a little of hell in it—no plan to retain this or that of the devil in our hearts or our pockets. Out Satan must go, every hair and feather!

[113] *Christ Our Righteousness*

Christ is our righteousness, not that we should escape punishment, still less escape being righteous, but as the live potent creator of righteousness in us, so that we, with our wills receiving His spirit, shall like Him resist unto blood, striving against sin.

[114] *Agree Quickly*

Arrange your matters with those who have anything against you, while you are yet together and things have not gone too far to be arranged; *you will have to do it,* and that under less easy circumstances than now. Putting off is of no use. You must. The thing has to be done; there are means of compelling you.

[115] *Duties to an Enemy*

It is a very small matter *to you* whether the man give you your right or not: it is life or death to you whether or not you give him his. Whether he pay you what you count his debt or no, you will be compelled to pay him all you owe him. If you owe him a pound and he you a million, you must pay him the pound whether he pay you the million or not; there is no business parallel here. If, owing you love, he gives you hate, you, owing him love, have yet to pay it.

[116] *The Prison*

I think I have seen from afar something of the final prison of all, the innermost cell of the debtor of the universe. . . . It is the vast outside; the ghastly dark beyond the gates of the city of which God is the light—where the evil dogs go ranging, silent as the dark, for there is no sound any more than sight. The time of signs is over. Every sense has (had) its signs, and they were all misused: there is no sense, no sign more—nothing now by means of which to believe. The man wakes from the final struggle of death, in absolute loneliness as in the most miserable moment of deserted childhood he never knew. Not a hint, not a shadow of anything outside his consciousness reaches him. . . . Soon misery will beget on his imagination a thousand shapes of woe, which he will not be able to rule, direct, or even distinguish from real presences.

[117] *Not Good to Be Alone*

In such evil case I believe the man would be glad to come in contact with the worst loathed insect: it would be a shape of life, something beyond and beside his own huge, void, formless being! I imagine some such feeling in the prayer of the devils for leave to go into the swine.... Without the correction, the reflection, the support of other presences, being is not merely unsafe, it is a horror—for anyone but God, who is His own being. For him whose idea is God's, and the image of God, his own being is far too fragmentary and imperfect to be anything like good company. It is the lovely creatures God has made all around us, in them giving us Himself, that, until we know Him, save us from the frenzy of aloneness—for that aloneness is self.

[118] *Be Ye Perfect*

Whoever will live must cease to be a slave and become a child of God. There is no halfway house of rest, where ungodliness may be dallied with, nor prove quite fatal. Be they few or many cast into such prison as I have endeavored to imagine, there can be no deliverance for human soul, whether in that prison or out of it, but in paying the last farthing, in becoming lowly, penitent, self-refusing—so receiving the sonship and learning to cry, *Father!*

[119] *The Heart*

And no scripture is of private interpretation, so is there no feeling in (a) human heart which exists in that heart alone—which is not, in some form or degree, in every heart.

[120] *Precious Blame*

No matter how His image may have been defaced in me, the thing defaced is His image, remains His defaced image—an image yet, that can hear His word. What makes me evil and miserable is that the thing spoiled in me is the image of the Perfect. Nothing can be evil but in virtue of a good hypostasis. No, no! Nothing can make it that I am not the child of God. If one say, "Look at the animals: God made them; you do not call them the children of God!" I answer, "But I am to blame: they are not to blame! I cling fast to my blame: it is the seal of my childhood." I have nothing to argue from in the animals, for I do not understand them. Two things I am sure of: that God is "a faithful creator" and that the sooner I put in force my claim to be a child of God, the better for them; for they too are fallen, though without blame.

[121]   *The Same*

However bad I may be, I am the child of God, and therein lies my blame. Ah, I would not lose my blame! In my blame lies my hope.

[122]   *Man Glorified*

Everything must at length be subject to man, as it was to The Man. When God can do what He will with a man, the man may do what he will with the world; he may walk on the sea like his Lord; the deadliest thing will not be able to hurt him.

[123] *Life in the Word*

All things were made *through* the Word, but that which was made *in* the Word was life, and that life is the light of men: they who live by this light, that is live as Jesus lived, by obedience, namely, to the Father, have a share in their own making; the light becomes life in them; they are, in their lower way, alive with the life that was first born in Jesus, and through Him has been born in them—by obedience they become one with the Godhead: "As many as received Him, to them gave He power to become the sons of God."

[124] *The Office of Christ*

Never could we have known the heart of the Father, never felt it possible to love Him as sons, but for Him who cast Himself into the gulf that yawned between us. In and through Him we were foreordained to the sonship: sonship, even had we never sinned, never could we reach without Him. We should have been little children loving the Father indeed, but children far from the sonhood that understands and adores.

[125]   *The Slowness of the New Creation*

As the world must be redeemed in a few men to begin with, so the soul is redeemed in a few of its thoughts, and works, and ways to begin with: it takes a long time to finish the new creation of this redemption.

[126]   *The New Creation*

When the sons of God show as they are, taking, with the character, the appearance and the place, that belong to their sonship; when the sons of God sit with *the* Son of God on the throne of their Father; then shall they be in potency of fact the lords of the lower creation, the bestowers of liberty and peace upon it: then shall the creation, subjected to vanity for their sakes, find its freedom in their freedom, its gladness in their sonship. The animals will glory to serve them, will joy to come to them for help. Let the heartless scoff, the unjust despise! the heart that cries *Abba, Father,* cries to the God of the sparrow and the oxen; nor can hope go too far in hoping what God will do for the creation that now groaneth and travaileth in pain because our higher birth is delayed.

[127] *Pessimism*

Low-sunk life imagines itself weary of life, but it is
death, not life, it is weary of.

[128] *The Work of the Father*

All things are possible with God, but all things are not
easy.... In the very nature of being—that is, God—it
must be hard—and divine history shows how hard—to
create that which shall be not Himself, yet like Himself.
The problem is, so far to separate from Himself that
which must yet on Him be ever and always and utterly
dependent, that it shall have the existence of an individ-
ual, and be able to turn and regard Him, choose Him,
and say "I will arise and go to my Father...." I imagine
the difficulty of doing this thing, of affecting this cre-
ation, this separation from Himself such that Will in
the creature shall be possible—I imagine, I say, that for
it God must begin inconceivably far back in the
infinitesimal regions of beginnings.

[129] *The End*

The final end of the separation is not individuality; that
is but a means to it: the final end is oneness — an impos-
sibility without it. For there can be no unity, no delight
of love, no harmony, no good in being, where there is
but one. Two at least are needed for oneness.

[130] *Deadlock*

Man finds it hard to get what he wants, because he does
not want the best; God finds it hard to give, because He
would give the best, and man will not take it.

[131] *The Two Worst Heresies*

The worst heresy, next to that of dividing religion and
righteousness, is to divide the Father from the Son;
. . . to represent the Son as doing that which the Father
does not Himself do.

[132]   *Christian Growth*

All the growth of the Christian is the more and more life he is receiving. At first his religion may hardly be distinguishable from the mere prudent desire to save his soul: but at last he loses that very soul in the glory of love, and so saves itself; self becomes but the cloud on which the white light of God divides into harmonies unspeakable.

[133]   *Life and Shadow*

Life is everything. Many doubtless mistake the joy of life for life itself, and, longing after the joy, languish with a thirst at once poor and inextinguishable; but even that, thirst points to the one spring. These love self, not life, and self is but the shadow of life. When it is taken for life itself, and set as the man's center, it becomes a live death in the man, a devil he worships as his God: the worm of the death eternal he clasps to his bosom as his one joy.

[134] *False Refuge*

Of all things let us avoid the false refuge of a weary collapse, a hopeless yielding to things as they are. It is the life in us that is discontented: we need more of what is discontented, not more of the cause of its discontent.

[135] *A Silly Notion*

No silly notion of playing the hero—what have creatures like us to do with heroism who are not yet barely honest?

[136] *Dryness*

The true man trusts in a strength which is not his, and which he does not feel, does not even always desire.

[137] *Perseverance*

To believe in the wide-awake real, through all the stu-
pefying, enervating, distorting dream: to will to wake,
when the very being seems athirst for Godless
repose:—these are the broken steps up to the high
fields where repose is but a form of strength, strength
but a form of joy, joy but a form of love.

[138] *The Lower Forms*

I trust that life in its lowest forms is on the way to
thought and blessedness, is in the process of that sepa-
ration, so to speak, from God, in which consists the
creation of living souls.

[139] *Life*

He who has it not cannot believe in it: how should
death believe in life, though all the birds of God are
singing jubilant over the empty tomb?

[140] *The Eternal Round*

Obedience is the joining of the links of the eternal round. Obedience is but the other side of the creative will. Will is God's will, obedience is man's will; the two make one. The root life, knowing well the thousand troubles it would bring upon Him, has created, and goes on creating, other lives, that though incapable of self-being they may, by willed obedience, share in the bliss of His essential self-ordained being. If we do the will of God, eternal life is ours—no mere continuity of existence, for that in itself is worthless as hell, but a being that is one with the essential life.

[141] *The Great One Life*

The infinite God, the great one life, than whom is no other—only shadows, lovely shadows of Him.

[142] *The Beginning of Wisdom*

Naturally the first emotion of man toward the being he calls God, but of whom he knows so little, is fear.

Where it is possible that fear should exist, it is well it should exist, cause continual uneasiness, and be cast out by nothing less than love. . . . Until love, which is the truth toward God, is able to cast out fear, it is well that fear should hold; it is a bond, however poor, between that which is and That which creates—a bond that must be broken, but a bond that can be broken only by the tightening of an infinitely closer bond. Verily God must be terrible to those that are far from Him: for they fear He will do, yea, He is doing with them what they do not, cannot desire, and can ill endure.

[143] *"Peace in Our Time"*

While they are such as they are, there is much in Him that cannot but affright them: they ought, they do well, to fear, Him. . . . To remove that fear from their hearts, save by letting them know His love with its purifying fire, a love which for ages, it may be, they cannot know, would be to give them up utterly to the power of evil. Persuade men that fear is a vile thing, that it is an insult to God, that He will none of it—while they are yet in love with their own will, and slaves to every movement of passionate impulse, and what will the consequence be? That they will insult God as a discarded idol, a superstition, a falsehood, as a thing under whose evil influence they have too long groaned, a thing to be cast out and spit upon. After that how much will they learn of Him?

[144] *Divine Fire*

The fire of God, which is His essential being, His love, His creative power, is a fire unlike its earthly symbol in this, that it is only at a distance it burns—that the further from Him, it burns the worse.

[145] *The Safe Place*

If then any child of the Father finds that he is afraid before Him, that the thought of God is a discomfort to him, or even a terror, let him make haste—let him not linger to put on any garment, but rush at once in his nakedness, a true child, for shelter from his own evil and God's terror, into the salvation of the Father's arms.

[146]   *God and Death*

All that is not God is death.

[147]   *Terror*

Endless must be our terror, until we come heart to heart with the fire-core of the universe, the first and the last of the living One.

[148]   *False Want*

Men who would rather receive salvation from God than God their salvation.

[149] *A Man's Right*

Lest it should be possible that any unchildlike soul
might, in arrogance and ignorance, think to stand upon
his rights *against* God, and demand of Him this or that
after the will of the flesh, I will lay before such a possi-
ble one some of the things to which he has a right. . . .
He has a claim to be compelled to repent; to be hedged
in on every side: to have one after another of the strong,
sharp-toothed sheep dogs of the Great Shepherd sent
after him, to thwart him in any desire, foil him in any
plan, frustrate him of any hope, until he come to see at
length that nothing will ease his pain, nothing make life
a thing worth having, but the presence of the living
God within him.

[150] *Nature*

In what belongs to the deeper meanings of nature and
her mediation between us and God, the appearances of
nature are the truths of nature, far deeper than any sci-
entific discoveries in and concerning them. The show
of things is that for which God cares *most*, for their
show is the face of far deeper things than they. . . . It is

through their show, not through their analysis, that we enter into their deepest truths. What they say to the childlike soul is the truest thing to be gathered of them. To know a primrose is a higher thing than to know all the botany of it—just as to know Christ is an infinitely higher thing than to know all theology, all that is said about His person, or babbled about His work. The body of man does not exist for the sake of its hidden secrets; its hidden secrets exist for the sake of its outside—for the face and the form in which dwells revelation: its outside is the deepest of it. So Nature as well exists primarily for her face, her look, her appeals to the heart and the imagination, her simple service to human need, and not for the secrets to be discovered in her and turned to man's further use.

[151]   *The Same*

By an infinite decomposition we should know nothing more of what a thing really is, for, the moment we decompose it, it ceases to be, and all its meaning is vanished. Infinitely more than astronomy even, which destroys nothing, can do for us, is done by the mere aspect and changes of the vault over our heads. Think for a moment what would be our idea of greatness, of God, of infinitude, of aspiration, if, instead of a blue, far withdrawn, light-spangled firmament, we were born and reared under a flat white ceiling! I would not be supposed to depreciate the labors of science, but I say its discoveries are unspeakably less precious than the merest gifts of Nature, those which, from morning to night, we take unthinking from her hands. One day, I trust, we shall be able to enter into their secrets from within them—by natural contact. . . .

[152]   *Doubt*

To deny the existence of God may . . . involve less unbelief than the smallest yielding to doubt of His goodness. I say *yielding;* for a man may be haunted with doubts, and only grow thereby in faith. Doubts are the messengers of the Living One to the honest. They are the first knock at our door of things that are not yet, but have to be, understood. . . . Doubt must precede every deeper assurance; for uncertainties are what we first see when we look into a region hitherto unknown, unexplored, unannexed.

[153] *Job*

Seeing God, Job forgets all he wanted to say, all he thought he would say if he could but see Him.

[154] *The Close of the Book of Job*

Job had his desire: he saw the face of God—and abhorred himself in dust and ashes. He sought justification; he found self-abhorrence.... Two things are clearly contained in, and manifest from, this poem:— that not every man deserves for his sins to be punished everlastingly from the presence of the Lord; and that the best of men, when he sees the face of God, will know himself vile. God is just, and will never deal with the sinner as if he were capable of sinning the pure sin; yet if the best man be not delivered from himself, that self will sink him into Tophet.

[155] *The Way*

Christ is the way out, and the way in: the way from slavery, conscious or unconscious, into liberty; the way

from the unhomeliness of things to the home we desire
but do not know; the way from the stormy skirts of the
Father's garments to the peace of His bosom.

[156] *Self-Control*

I will allow that the mere effort of will . . . may add to
the man's power over his lower nature; but in that very
nature it is God who must rule and not the man, how
very well he may mean. From a man's rule of himself in
smallest opposition, however devout, to the law of his
being, arises the huge danger of nourishing, by the
pride of self-conquest, a far worse than even the
unchained animal self—the demoniac self. True victory
over self is the victory of God in the man, not of the
man alone. It is not subjugation that is enough, but
subjugation by God. In whatever man does without
God, he must fail miserably—or succeed more miser-
ably. No portion of a man can rule another, for God,
not the man, created it, and the part is greater than the
whole. . . . The diseased satisfaction which some minds
feel in laying burdens on themselves, is a pampering,
little as they may suspect it, of the most dangerous

appetite of that self which they think they are morti-
fying.

[157] *Self-Denial*

The self is given to us that we may sacrifice it: it is ours,
that we, like Christ, may have somewhat to offer—not
that we should torment it, but that we should deny it;
not that we should cross it, but that we should abandon
it utterly: then it can no more be vexed. "What can this
mean?—we are not to thwart, but to abandon?" . . . It
means this:—we must refuse, abandon, deny self alto-
gether as a ruling, or determining, or originating ele-
ment in us. It is to be no longer the regent of our action.
We are no more to think "What should I like to do?"
but "What would the Living One have me do?"

[158] *Killing the Nerve*

No grasping or seeking, no hungering of the individual,
shall give motion to the will: no desire to be conscious
of worthiness shall order the life; no ambition whatever

shall be a motive of action; no wish to surpass another be allowed a moment's respite from death.

[159] *Self*

Self, I have not to consult you but Him whose idea is the soul of you, and of which as yet you are all unworthy. I have to do, not with you, but with the Source of you, by whom it is that (at) any moment you exist—the Causing of you, not the caused you. You may be my consciousness but you are not my being. . . . For God is more to me than my consciousness of myself. He is my life; you are only so much of it as my poor half-made being can grasp—as much of it as I can now know at once. Because I have fooled and spoiled you, treated you as if you were indeed my own self, you have dwindled yourself and have lessened me, till I am ashamed of myself. If I were to mind what you say, I should soon be sick of you; even now I am ever and anon disgusted with your paltry mean face, which I meet at every turn. No! Let me have the company of the Perfect One, not of you! Of my elder brother, the Living One! I will not make a friend of the mere shadow of my own being!

Good-bye, Self! I deny you, and will do my best every day to leave you behind.

[160]   *My Yoke Is Easy*

The will of the Father is the yoke He would have us take, and bear also with Him. It is of this yoke that he says *It is easy*, of this burden, *It is light*. He is not saying "The yoke I lay upon you is easy, the burden light"; what He says is, "The yoke I carry is easy, the burden on My shoulders is light." With the garden of Gethsemane before Him, with the hour and the power of darkness waiting for Him, He declares His yoke is easy, His burden light.

[161]   *We Must Be Jealous*

We must be jealous for God against ourselves and look well to the cunning and deceitful self—ever cunning and deceitful until it is informed of God—until it is thoroughly and utterly denied. . . . Until then its very denials, its very turnings from things dear to it for the sake of Christ, will tend to foster its self-regard, and generate in it a yet deeper self-worship.

[162]   *Facing Both Ways*

Is there not many a Christian who, having *begun* to deny himself, yet spends much strength in the vain and evil endeavor to accommodate matters between Christ and the dear Self—seeking to save that which so he must certainly lose—in how different a way from that in which the Master would have him lose it!

[163]   *The Careless Soul*

The careless soul receives the Father's gifts as if it were a way things had of dropping into his hand . . . yet is he ever complaining, as if someone were accountable for the checks which meet him at every turn. For the good that comes to him, he gives no thanks—who is there to thank? At the disappointments that befall him he grumbles—there must be someone to blame!

[164]   *There Is No Merit in It*

In the main we love because we cannot help it. There is
no merit in it: how should there be any love? But nei-
ther is it selfish. There are many who confound righ-
teousness with merit, and think there is nothing
righteous where there is nothing meritorious. "If it
makes you happy to love," they say, "where is your
merit? It is only selfishness." There is no merit, I reply,
yet the love that is born in us is our salvation from self-
ishness. It is of the very essence of righteousness. . . .
That *certain* joys should be joys, is the very denial of
selfishness. The man would be a demoniacally selfish
man, whom Love itself did not make joyful.

[165]   *Faith*

Do you ask, "What is faith in Him?" I answer, The
leaving of your way, your objects, your self, and the
taking of His and Him; the leaving of your trust in
men, in money, in opinion, in character, in atonement
itself, *and doing as He tells you.* I can find no words
strong enough to serve for the weight of this obedience.

[166]   *The Misguided*

Instead of so knowing Christ that they have Him in them saving them, they lie wasting themselves in soul-sickening self-examination as to whether they are believers, whether they are really trusting in the atonement, whether they are truly sorry for their sins—the way to madness of the brain, and despair of the heart.

[167]   *The Way*

Instead of asking yourself whether you believe or not, ask yourself whether you have this day done one thing because He said, *Do it,* or once abstained because He said, *Do not do it.* It is simply absurd to say you believe, or even want to believe, in Him, if you do not do anything He tells you.

[168]   *The First and Second Persons*

I worship the Son as the human God, the divine, the only, Man, deriving His being and power from the Father, equal with Him as a son is the equal at once and the subject of his father.

[169]   *Warning*

We must not wonder things away into nonentity.

[170]   *Creation*

The word *creation* applied to the loftiest success of human genius, seems to me a mockery of humanity, itself in process of creation.

[171]   *The Unknowable*

As to what the life of God is to Himself, we can only know that we cannot know it—even that not being absolute ignorance, for no one can see that, from its very nature, he cannot understand a thing without therein approaching that thing in a most genuine manner.

[172] *Warning*

Let us understand very plainly, that a being whose essence was only power would be such a negation of the divine that no righteous worship could be offered him.

[173] *The Two First Persons*

The response to self-existent love is self-abnegating love. The refusal of Himself is that in Jesus which corresponds to the creation in God. . . . When he died on the cross, He did that, in the wild weather of His outlying provinces, in the torture of the body of His revelation, which He had done at home in glory and gladness.

[174] *The Imitation of Christ*

There is no life for any man other than the same kind that Jesus has; His disciples must live by the same absolute devotion of his will to the Father's: then is his life one with the life of the Father.

[175] *Pain and Joy*

The working out of this our salvation must be pain, and the handling of it down to them that are below must ever be in pain; but the eternal form of the will of God in and for us, is intensity of bliss.

[176] *"By Him All Things Consist"*

The bond of the universe . . . is the devotion of the Son to the Father. It is the life of the universe. It is not the fact that God created all things, that makes the universe a whole; but that He through Whom He created them loves Him perfectly, is eternally content in His Father, is satisfied to be because His Father is with Him. It is not the fact that God is all in all that unites the universe: it is the love of the Son to the Father. For of no one-hood comes unity; there can be no oneness where there is only one. For the very beginnings of unity there must be two. Without Christ therefore there could be no universe.

[177]   *"In Him Was Life"*

We too must have life in ourselves. We too must, like
the Life Himself, live. We can live in no way but that in
which Jesus lived, in which life was made in Him. The
way is, to give up our life. . . . Till then we are not alive;
life is not made in us. The whole strife and labor and
agony of the Son with every man is to get him to die as
He died. All preaching that aims not at this is a building
with wood, and hay, and stubble.

[178]   *Why We Have Not Christ's*
"Ipsissima Verba"

God has not cared that we should anywhere have
assurance of His very words; and that not merely per-
haps, because of the tendency in His children to word-
worship, false logic, and corruption of the truth, but
because He would not have them oppressed by words,
seeing that words, being human, therefore but partially
capable, could not absolutely contain or express what
the Lord meant, and that even He must depend for
being understood upon the spirit of His disciple.

Seeing it could not give life, the letter should not be throned with power to kill.

[179] *Warning*

"How am I to know that a thing is true?" By *doing* what you know to be true, and calling nothing true until you see it to be true; by shutting your mouth until the truth opens it. Are you meant to be silent? Then woe to you if you speak.

[180] *On Bad Religious Art*

If the Lord were to appear this day in England as once in Palestine, He would not come in the halo of the painters or with that wintry shine of effeminate beauty, of sweet weakness, in which it is their helpless custom to represent Him.

[181] *How to Read the Epistles*

The uncertainty lies always in the intellectual region, never in the practical. What Paul cares about is plain enough to the true heart, however far from plain to the man whose desire to understand goes ahead of his obedience.

[182] *The Entrance of Christ*

When we receive His image into our spiritual mirror, He enters with it. Our thought is not cut off from His. Our open receiving thought is His door to come in. When our hearts turn to Him, that is opening the door to Him, that is holding up our mirror to Him; then He comes in, not by our thought only, not in our idea only, but He comes Himself and of His own will—comes in as we could not take Him, but as He can come.

[183] *The Same*

Thus the Lord ... becomes the soul of our souls, becomes spiritually what He always was creatively;

and as our spirit informs, gives shape to, our bodies, in like manner His soul informs, gives shape to, our souls. The deeper soul that willed and wills our souls rises up, the infinite Life, into the Self we call *I* and *me,* but which lives immediately from Him and is His very own property and nature—unspeakably more His than ours ... until at length the glory of our existence flashes upon us, we face full to the sun that enlightens what it sent forth, and know ourselves alive with an infinite life, even the Life of the Father; know that our existence is not the moonlight of a mere consciousness of being but the sun-glory of a life justified by having become one with its origin, thinking and feeling with the primal Sun of life, from whom it was dropped away that it might know and bethink itself and return to circle forever in exultant harmony around Him.

[184] *The Uses of Nature*

What notion should we have of the unchanging and unchangeable, without the solidity of matter? . . . How should we imagine what we may of God without the firmament over our heads, a visible sphere, yet a formless infinitude? What idea could we have of God without the sky?

[185] *Natural Science*

Human science is but the backward undoing of the tapestry-web of God's science, works with its back to Him, and is always leaving Him—His intent, that is, His perfected work—behind it, always going farther and farther away from the point where His work culminates in revelation.

[186] *The Value of Analysis*

Analysis is well, as death is well.

[187]   *Nature*

The truth of the flower is, not the facts about it, be they
correct as ideal science itself, but the shining, glowing,
gladdening, patient thing throned on its stalk—the
compeller of smile and tear. . . . The idea of God *is* the
flower: His idea is not the botany of the flower. Its
botany is but a thing of ways and means—of canvas
and color and brush in relation to the picture in the
painter's brain.

[188]   *Water*

Is oxygen-and-hydrogen the divine idea of water? God
put the two together only that man might separate and
find them out? He allows His child to pull his toys to
pieces: but were they made that he might pull them
to pieces? He were a child not to be envied for whom
his inglorious father would make toys to such an end!
A school examiner might see therein the best use of a
toy, but not a father! Find for us what in the constitu-
tion of the two gases makes them fit and capable to be
thus honored in forming the lovely thing, and you will
give us a revelation about more than water, namely

about the God who made oxygen and hydrogen. There is no water in oxygen, no water in hydrogen; it comes bubbling fresh from the imagination of the living God, rushing from under the great white throne of the glacier. The very thought of it makes one gasp with an elemental joy no metaphysician can analyze. The water itself, that dances and sings, and slakes the wonderful thirst—symbol and picture of that draught for which the woman of Samaria made her prayer to Jesus—this lovely thing itself, whose very witness is a delight to every inch of the human body in its embrace—this live thing which, if I might, I would have running through my room, yea, babbling along my table—this water is its own self its own truth, and is therein a truth of God. Let him who would know the truth of the Maker, become sorely athirst, and drink of the brook by the way—then lift up his heart—not at that moment to the Maker of oxygen and hydrogen, but to the Inventor and Mediator of thirst and water, that man might foresee a little of what his soul might find in God.

[189] *Truth of Things*

The truth *of a thing*, then, is the blossom of it, the thing
it is made for, the topmost stone set on with rejoicing;
truth in a man's imagination is the power to recognize
this truth of a thing.

[190] *Caution*

But far higher will the doing of the least, the most
insignificant, duty raise him.

[191] *Duties*

These relations are facts of man's nature. . . . He is so
constituted as to understand them at first more than he
can love them, with the resulting advantage of having
thereby the opportunity of choosing them purely
because they are true: so doing he chooses to love them,
and is enabled to love them in the doing, which alone
can truly reveal them to him and make the loving of
them possible. Then they cease to show themselves in
the form of duties and appear as they more truly are,

absolute truths, essential realities, eternal delights. The man is a true man who chooses duty: he is a perfect man who at length never thinks of duty, who forgets the name of it.

[192] *Why Free Will Was Permitted*

One who went to the truth by mere impulse would be a holy animal, not a true man. Relations, truths, duties, are shown to the man away beyond him, that he may *choose* them and be a child of God, choosing righteousness like Him. Hence the whole sad victorious human tale and the glory to be revealed.

[193] *Eternal Death*

Not fulfilling these relations, the man is undoing the right of his own existence, destroying his *raison d'être*, making of himself a monster, a live reason why he should not live.

[194] *The Redemption of Our Nature*

When (a man) is aware of an opposition in him, which is not harmony: that, while he hates it, there is yet present with him, and seeming to be himself, what sometimes he calls *the old Adam,* sometimes *the flesh,* sometimes *his lower nature,* sometimes *his evil self;* and sometimes recognizes as simply that part of his being where God is not; then indeed is the man in the region of truth, and beginning to come true in himself. Nor will it be long ere he discover that there is no part in him with which he would be at strife, so God were there, so that it were true, what it ought to be—in right relation to the whole; for, by whatever name called, the old Adam, or antecedent horse, or dog, or tiger, it would then fulfill its part holily, intruding upon nothing, subject utterly to the rule of the higher; horse, or dog, or tiger, it would be good horse, good dog, good tiger.

[195]   *No Mystery*

Man bows down before a power that can account for him, a power to whom he is no mystery as he is to himself.

[196]   *The Live Truth*

When a man is, with his whole nature, loving and willing the truth, he is then a live truth. But this he has not originated in himself. He has seen it and striven for it, but not originated it. The more originating, living, visible truth, embracing all truths in all relations, is Jesus Christ. He is true: He is the live Truth.

[197]   *Likeness to Christ*

His likeness to Christ is the truth of a man, even as the perfect meaning of a flower is the truth of a flower. . . . As Christ is the blossom of humanity, so the blossom of every man is the Christ perfected in him.

[198] *Grace and Freedom*

He gives us the will wherewith to will, and the power
to use it, and the help needed to supplement the power:
... but we ourselves must will the truth and for that the
Lord is waiting.... The work is His, but we must take
our willing share. When the blossom breaks forth in us,
the more it is ours the more it is His.

[199] *Glorious Liberty*

When a man is true, if he were in hell he could not be
miserable. He is right with himself because right with
Him whence he came. To be right with God is to be
right with the universe: one with the power, the love,
the will of the mighty Father, the cherisher of joy, the
Lord of laughter, whose are all glories, all hopes, who
loves everything and hates nothing but selfishness.

[200] *No Middle Way*

There is, in truth, no mid way between absolute har-
mony with the Father and the condition of slaves—

submissive or rebellious. If the latter, their very rebellion is by the strength of the Father in them.

[201]   *On Having One's Own Way*

The liberty of the God who would have his creatures free, is in contest with the slavery of the creature who would cut his own stem from his root that he might call it his own and love it; who rejoices in his own consciousness, instead of the life of that consciousness; who poises himself on the tottering wall of his own being, instead of the rock on which that being is built. Such a one regards his own dominion over himself— the rule of the greater by the less—as a freedom infinitely larger than the range of the universe of God's being. If he says, "At least I have it in my own way!", I answer, you do not know what is your way and what is not. You know nothing of whence your impulses, your desires, your tendencies, your likings come. They may spring now from some chance, as of nerves diseased; now from some roar of a wandering bodiless devil; now from some infant hate in your heart; now from the greed of lawlessness of some ancestor you would be ashamed of if you knew him; or, it may be, now from some far-piercing chord of a heavenly orchestra: the moment comes up into your consciousness, you call it your own way, and glory in it.

[202]   *The Death of Christ*

Christ died to save us, not from suffering, but from ourselves; not from injustice, far less from justice, but from being unjust. He died that we might live—but live as He lives, by dying as He died who died to Himself.

[203]   *Hell*

The one principle of hell is—"I am my own!"

[204]   *The Lie*

To all these principles of hell, or of this world—they are the same thing, and it matters nothing whether they are asserted or defended so long as they are acted upon—the Lord, the King, gives the direct lie.

[205] *The Author's Fear*

If I mistake, He will forgive me. I do not fear Him: I fear only lest, able to see and write these things, I should fail of witnessing and myself be, after all, a castaway—no king but a talker; no disciple of Jesus, ready to go with Him to the death, but an arguer about the truth.

[206] *Sincerity*

We are not bound to say all we think but we are bound not even to look what we do not think.

[207] *First Things First*

Oh the folly of any mind that would explain God before obeying Him! That would map out the character of God instead of crying, Lord, what wouldst thou have me to do?

[208] *Inexorable Love*

A man might flatter, or bribe, or coax a tyrant; but there is no refuge from the love of God; that love will, for very love, insist upon the uttermost farthing. — "That is not the sort of love I care about!" — No; how should you? I well believe it.

[209] *Salvation*

The notion that the salvation of Jesus is a salvation from the consequences of our sins is a false, mean, low notion.... Jesus did not die to save us from punishment; He was called Jesus because He should save His people from their sins.

[210] *Charity and Orthodoxy*

Every man who tries to obey the Master is my brother, whether he counts me such or not, and I revere him; but dare I give quarter to what I see to be a lie because my brother believes it? The lie is not of God, whoever may hold it.

[211] *Evasion*

To put off obeying Him till we find a credible theory concerning Him is to set aside the potion we know it our duty to drink, for the study of the various schools of therapy.

[212] *Inexorable Love*

Such is the mercy of God that He will hold His children in the consuming fire of His distance until they pay the uttermost farthing, until they drop the purse of selfishness with all the dross that is in it, and rush home to the Father and the Son and the many brethren—rush inside the center of the life-giving fire whose outer circles burn.

[213] *The Holy Ghost*

To him who obeys, and thus opens the door of his heart to receive the eternal gift, God gives the Spirit of His Son, the Spirit of Himself, to be in him, and lead him to the understanding of all truth. . . . The true disciple shall thus always know what he ought to do, though not necessarily what another ought to do.

[214]   *The Sense of Sin*

Sense of sin is not inspiration, though it may lie not far from the temple door. It is indeed an opener of the eyes, but upon home defilement, not upon heavenly truth.

[215]   *Mean Theologies*

They regard the Father of their spirits as their governor! They yield the idea of ... "the glad Creator," and put in its stead a miserable, puritanical, martinet of a God, caring not for righteousness but for His rights: not for the eternal purities, but the goody proprieties. The prophets of such a God take all the glow, all the hope, all the color, all the worth, out of life on earth, and offer you instead what they call eternal bliss—a pale, tearless hell. ... But if you are straitened in your own mammon-worshipping soul, how shall you believe in a God any greater than can stand up in that prison chamber?

[216]   *On Believing Ill of God*

Neither let thy cowardly conscience receive any word as light because another call it light, while it looks to thee dark. Say either the thing is not what it seems, or God never said or did it. But of all evils, to misinterpret what God does, and then say the thing, as interpreted, must be right because God does it, is of the devil. Do not try to believe anything that affects thee as darkness. Even if thou mistake and refuse something true thereby, thou wilt do less wrong to Christ by such a refusal than thou wouldst by accepting as His what thou canst see only as darkness . . . but let thy words be few, lest thou say with thy tongue what thou wilt afterward repent with thy heart.

[217]   *Condemnation*

No man is condemned for anything he has done: he is condemned for continuing to do wrong. He is condemned for not coming out of the darkness, for not coming to the light.

[218]   *Excuses*

As soon as a man begins to make excuse, the time has come when he might be doing that from which he excuses himself.

[219]   *Impossibilities*

"I thank thee, Lord, for forgiving me, but I prefer staying in the darkness: forgive me that too."—"No; that cannot be. The one thing that cannot be forgiven is the sin of choosing to be evil, of refusing deliverance. It is impossible to forgive that. It would be to take part in it."

[220] *Disobedience*

How many are there not who seem capable of anything for the sake of the Church or Christianity, except the one thing its Lord cares about—that they should do what He tells them. He would deliver them from themselves into the liberty of the sons of God, make them His brothers: they leave Him to vaunt their Church.

[221] *The Same*

To say a man might disobey and be none the worse would be to say that *no* might be *yes* and light sometimes darkness.

[222] *The God of Remembrance*

I do not mean that God would have even His closest presence make us forget or cease to desire that of our friend. God forbid! The Love of God is the perfecting of every love. He is not the God of oblivion but of eternal remembrance. There is no past with Him.

[223] *Bereavement*

"Ah, you little know my loss!" — "Indeed it is great! It seems to include God! If you knew what He knows about death you would clap your listless hands. But why should I seek in vain to comfort you? You must be made miserable that you may wake from your sleep to know that you need God. If you do not find Him, endless life with the living (being) whom you bemoan would become and remain to you unendurable. The knowledge of your own heart will teach you this: — not the knowledge you have, but the knowledge that is on its way to you through suffering. Then you will feel that existence itself is the prime of evils without the righteousness that is of God by faith."

[224] *Abraham's Faith*

The Apostle says that a certain thing was imputed to Abraham for righteousness: or, as the revised version has it, "reckoned unto him": what was it that was thus imputed to Abraham? The righteousness of another? God forbid! It was his own faith. The faith of Abraham is reckoned to him for righteousness.

[225]   *The Same*

Paul says faith in God was counted righteousness before Moses was born. You may answer, Abraham was unjust in many things, and by no means a righteous man. True: he was not a righteous man in any complete sense. His righteousness would never have satisfied Paul; neither, you may be sure, did it satisfy Abraham. But his faith was nevertheless righteousness.

[226]   *Perception of Duties*

You may say this is not one's first feeling of duty. True: but the first in reality is seldom the first perceived. The first duty is too high and too deep to come first into consciousness. If anyone were born perfect ... the highest duty would come first into the consciousness. As we are born, it is the doing of, or at least the honest trying to do many another duty, that will at length lead a man to see that his duty to God is the first and deepest and highest of all, including and requiring the performance of all other duties whatever.

[227] *Righteousness of Faith*

To the man who has no faith in God, faith in God cannot look like righteousness; neither can he know that it is creative of all other righteousness toward equal and inferior lives.

[228] *The Same*

It is not like some single separate act of righteousness: it is the action of the whole man, turning to good from evil—turning his back on all that is opposed to righteousness, and starting on a road on which he cannot stop, in which he must go on growing more and more righteous, discovering more and more what righteousness is, and more and more what is unrighteous in himself.

[229] *Reckoned unto Us for Righteousness*

With what life and possibility is in him, he must keep turning to righteousness and abjuring iniquity, ever aiming at the righteousness of God. Such an obedient faith is most justly and fairly, being all that God Himself can require of the man, called by God righteousness in the man. It would not be enough for the righteousness of God, or Jesus, or any perfected saint, because they are capable of perfect righteousness.

[230]   St. Paul's Faith

His faith was an act recognizing God as his law, and that is not a partial act, but an all-embracing and all-determining action. A single righteous deed toward one's fellow could hardly be imputed to a man as righteousness. A man who is not trying after righteousness may yet do many a righteous act: they will not be forgotten to him, neither will they be imputed to him as righteousness.

[231]   The Full-Grown Christian

He does not take his joy from himself. He feels joy in himself, but it comes to him from others, not from

himself—from God first, and from somebody, any-
body, everybody next. . . . He could do without know-
ing himself, but he could not know himself and spare
one of the brothers or sisters God has given him. . . .
His consciousness of himself is the reflex from those
about him, not the result of his own turning in of his
regard upon himself. It is not the contemplation of
what God had made him, it is the being what God has
made him, and the contemplation of what God him-
self is, and what He has made his fellows, that gives
him his joy.

[232] *Revealed to Babes*

The wise and prudent must make a system and arrange
things to his mind before he can say, *I believe.* The
child sees, believes, obeys—and knows he must be per-
fect as his Father in heaven is perfect. If an angel, seem-
ing to come from heaven, told him that God had let
him off, that He did not require so much of him, but
would be content with less . . . the child would at once
recognize, woven with the angel's starry brilliancy, the
flicker of the flames of hell.

[233] *Answer*

"But how can God bring this about in me?"—Let Him
do it and perhaps you will know.

[234] *Useless Knowledge*

To teach your intellect what has to be learned by your
whole being, what cannot be understood without the
whole being, what it would do you no good to under-
stand save you understood it in your whole being—if
this be the province of any man, it is not mine. Let the
dead bury their dead, and the dead teach their dead.

[235] *The Art of Being Created*

Let patience have her perfect work. Statue under the
chisel of the sculptor, stand steady to the blows of his
mallet. Clay on the wheel, let the fingers of the divine
potter model you at their will. Obey the Father's light-
est word: hear the Brother who knows you and died
for you.

[236] *When We Do Not Find Him*

Thy hand be on the latch to open the door at His first knock. Shouldst thou open the door and not see Him, do not say He did not knock, but understand that He is there, and wants thee to go out to Him. It may be He has something for thee to do for Him. Go and do it, and perhaps thou wilt return with a new prayer, to find a new window in thy soul.

[237] *Prayer*

Never wait for fitter time or place to talk to Him. To wait till thou go to church or to thy closet is to make Him wait. He will listen as thou walkest.

[238] *On One's Critics*

Do not heed much if men mock you and speak lies of you, or in goodwill defend you unworthily. Heed not much if even the righteous turn their backs upon you. Only take heed that you turn not from them.

[239]   *Free Will*

He gave man the power to thwart His will, that, by means of that same power, he might come at last to do His will in a higher kind and way than would otherwise have been possible to him.

[240]   *On Idle Tongues*

Let a man do right, not trouble himself about worthless opinion; the less he heeds tongues, the less difficult will he find it to love men.

[241]   *Do We Love Light?*

Do you so love the truth and the right that you welcome, or at least submit willingly to, the idea of an exposure of what in you is yet unknown to yourself—an exposure that may redound to the glory of the truth by making you ashamed and humble? . . . Are you willing to be made glad that you were wrong when you thought others were wrong?

[242] Shame

We may trust God with our past as heartily as with our future. It will not hurt us so long as we do not try to hide things, so long as we are ready to bow our heads in hearty shame where it is fit we should be ashamed. For to be ashamed is a holy and blessed thing. Shame is a thing to shame only those who want to appear, not those who want to be. Shame is to shame those who want to pass their examination, not those who would get into the heart of things. . . . To be humbly ashamed is to be plunged in the cleansing bath of truth.

[243] The Wakening

What a horror will it not be to a vile man . . . when his eyes are opened to see himself as the pure see him, as God sees him! Imagine such a man waking all at once, not only to see the eyes of the universe fixed upon him with loathing astonishment, but to see himself at the same moment as those eyes see him.

[244] *The Wakening of the Rich*

What riches and fancied religion, with the self-suffi-
ciency they generate between them, can make man or
woman capable of, is appalling. . . . To many of the reli-
gious rich in that day, the great damning revelation will
be their behavior to the poor to whom they thought
themselves very kind.

[245] *Self-Deception*

A man may loathe a thing in the abstract for years, and
find at last that all the time he has been, in his own per-
son, guilty of it. To carry a thing under our cloak
caressingly, hides from us its identity with something
that stands before us on the public pillory. Many a man
might read this and assent to it, who cages in his own
bosom a carrion bird that he never knows for what it is,
because there are points of difference in its plumage
from that of the bird he calls by an ugly name.

[246] *Warning*

"Oh God," we think, "How terrible if it were I!" Just so terrible is it that it should be Judas. And have I not done things with the same germ in them, a germ which, brought to its evil perfection, would have shown itself the cankerworm, treachery? Except I love my neighbor as myself, I may one day betray him! Let us therefore be compassionate and humble, and hope for every man.

[247] *The Slow Descent*

A man may sink by such slow degrees that, long after he is a devil, he may go on being a good churchman or a good dissenter and thinking himself a good Christian.

[248] *Justice and Revenge*

While a satisfied justice is an unavoidable eternal event, a satisfied revenge is an eternal impossibility.

[249]   *Recognition Hereafter*

Our friends will know us then; for their joy, will it be,
or their sorrow? Will their hearts sink within them
when they look on the real likeness of us? Or will they
rejoice to find that we were not so much to be blamed
as they thought?

[250]   *From Dante*

To have a share in any earthly inheritance is to diminish
the share of the other inheritors. In the inheritance of
the saints, that which each has goes to increase the pos-
session of the rest.

[251]   *What God Means by "Good"*

"They are good"; that is, "They are what I mean."

[252] *All Things from God*

All things are God's, not as being in His power—that of course—but as coming from Him. The darkness itself becomes light around Him when we think that verily He hath created the darkness, for there could have been no darkness but for the light.

[253] *Absolute Being*

There is no word to represent that which is not God, no word for the *where* without God in it; for it is not, could not be.

[254] *Beasts*

The ways of God go down into microscopic depths as well as up to telescopic heights.... So with mind; the ways of God go into the depths yet unrevealed to us: He knows His horses and dogs as we cannot know them, because we are not yet pure sons of God. When through our sonship, as Paul teaches, the redemption of these lower brothers and sisters shall have come, then we shall understand each other better. But now the Lord of Life has to look on at the willful torture of multitudes of His creatures. It must be that offenses come, but woe unto that man by whom they come! The Lord may seem not to heed, but He sees and knows.

[255] *Diversity of Souls*

Every one of us is something that the other is not, and therefore knows something—it may be without knowing that he knows it—which no one else knows: and . . . it is everyone's business, as one of the kingdom of light and inheritor in it all, to give his portion to the rest.

[256] *The Disillusioned*

Loving but the body of Truth, even here they come to call it a lie, and break out in maudlin moaning over the illusions of life.

[257] *Evil*

What springs from myself and not from God is evil: It is a perversion of something of God's. Whatever is not of faith is sin; it is a stream cut off—a stream that cuts itself off from its source and thinks to run on without it.

[258] *The Loss of the Shadow*

I learned that it was not myself but only my shadow that I had lost. I learned that it is better . . . for a proud man to fall and be humbled than to hold up his head in pride and fancied innocence. I learned that he that will be a hero, will barely be a man; that he that will be nothing but a doer of his work, is sure of his manhood.

[259] *Love*

It is by loving and not by being loved that one can come nearest to the soul of another.

[260] *From Spring to Summer*

The birds grew silent, because their history laid hold on them, compelling them to turn their words into deeds, and keep eggs warm, and hunt for worms.

[261] *The Door into Life*

But the door into life generally opens behind us, and a hand is put forth which draws us in backwards. The sole wisdom for man or boy who is haunted with the hovering of unseen wings, with the scent of unseen roses, and the subtle enticements of "melodies unheard," is *work*. If he follow any of those, they will vanish. But if he work, they will come unsought.

[262] *A Lonely Religion*

There is one kind of religion in which the more devoted a man is, the fewer proselytes he makes: the worship of himself.

[263] *Love*

Love makes everything lovely: hate concentrates itself on the one thing hated.

[264] *A False Method*

It is not by driving away our brother that we can be alone with God.

[265] *Assimilation*

All wickedness tends to destroy individuality and declining natures assimilate as they sink.

[266] *Looking*

"But ye was luikin' for somebody, auntie." — "Na. I was only jist luikin'." ... It is this formless idea of something at hand that keeps men and women striving to tear from the bosom of the world the secret of their own hopes. How little they know that what they look for in reality is their God!

[267]   *Progress*

To tell the truth, I feel a good deal younger. For then I only knew that a man had to take up his cross; whereas now I know that a man has to follow Him.

[268]   *Providence*

People talk about special providences. I believe in the providences, but not in the specialty. . . . The so-called special providences are no exception to the rule—they are common to all men at all moments.

[269]   *Ordinariness*

That which is best He gives most plentifully, as is reason with Him. Hence the quiet fullness of ordinary nature; hence the Spirit to them that ask it.

[270] *Forgiveness*

I prayed to God that He would make me . . . into a rock
which swallowed up the waves of wrong in its great
caverns and never threw them back to swell the com-
motion of the angry sea whence they came. Ah, what it
would be actually to annihilate wrong in this way—to
be able to say, "It shall not be wrong against me, so
utterly do I forgive it!" . . . But the painful fact will
show itself, not less curious than painful, that it is more
difficult to forgive small wrongs than great ones.
Perhaps, however, the forgiveness of the great wrongs
is not so true as it seems. For do we not think it a fine
thing to forgive such wrongs and so do it rather for
our own sakes than for the sake of the wrongdoer? It
is dreadful not to be good, and to have bad ways
inside one.

[271] *Visitors*

By all means tell people, when you are busy about
something that must be done, that you cannot spare the
time for them except they want of you something of
yet more pressing necessity; but *tell* them, and do not

get rid of them by the use of the instrument commonly called *the cold shoulder.* It is a wicked instrument.

[272]   *Prose*

My own conviction is that the poetry is far the deepest in us and that the prose is only broken-down poetry; and likewise that to this our lives correspond.... As you will hear some people read poetry so that no mortal could tell it was poetry, so do some people read their own lives and those of others.

[273]   *Integrity*

I would not favor a fiction to keep a whole world out of hell. The hell that a lie would keep any man out of is doubtless the very best place for him to go to. It is truth ... that saves the world!

[274]   *Contentment*

Let me, if I may, be ever welcomed to my room in win-
ter by a glowing hearth, in summer by a vase of flowers;
if I may not, let me think how nice they would be, and
bury myself in my work. I do not think that the road to
contentment lies in despising what we have not got. Let
us acknowledge all good, all delight that the world
holds, and be content without it.

[275]   *Psychical Research*

Offered the Spirit of God for the asking . . . they betake
themselves to necromancy instead, and raise the dead
to ask their advice, and follow it, and will find some day
that Satan had not forgotten how to dress like an angel
of light. . . . What religion is there in being convinced of
a future state? Is that to worship God? It is no more
religion than the belief that the sun will rise tomorrow
is religion. It may be a source of happiness to those
who could not believe it before, but it is not religion.

[276]   *The Blotting Out*

If He pleases to forget anything, then He can forget it.
And I think that is what He does with our sins—that is,
after He has got them away from us, once we are clean
from them altogether. It would be a dreadful thing if
He forgot them before that. . . .

[277]   *On a Chapter in Isaiah*

The power of God is put side by side with the weakness
of men, not that He, the perfect, may glory over His
feeble children . . . but that He may say thus: "Look,
my children, you will never be strong with *my*
strength. I have no other to give you."

[278]   *Providence*

And if we believe that God is everywhere, why should
we not think Him present even in the coincidences that
sometimes seem so strange? For, if He be in the things
that coincide, He must be in the coincidence of those
things.

[279] *No Other Way*

The Old Man of the Earth stooped over the floor of the cave, raised a huge stone, and left it leaning. It disclosed a great hole that went plumb-down. "That is the way," he said. "But there are no stairs. You must throw yourself in. There is no other way."

[280] *Death*

"You have tasted of death now," said the Old Man. "Is it good?" "It is good," said Mossy. "It is better than life." "No," said the Old Man. "It is only more life."

[281] *Criterion of a True Vision*

This made it the more likely that he had seen a true vision; for instead of making common things look commonplace, as a false vision would have done, it had made common things disclose the wonderful that was in them.

[282] *One Reason for Sex*

One of the great goods that come of having two parents is that the one balances and rectifies the motions of the other. No one is good but God. No one holds the truth, or can hold it, in one and the same thought, but God. Our human life is often, at best, but an oscillation between the extremes which together make the truth.

[283] *Easy Work*

Do you think the work God gives us to do is never easy? Jesus says His yoke is easy, His burden is light. People sometimes refuse to do God's work just because it is easy. This is sometimes because they cannot believe that easy work is His work; but there may be a very bad pride in it. . . . Some, again, accept it with half a heart and do it with half a hand. But however easy any work may be, it cannot be well done without taking thought about it. And such people, instead of taking thought about their work, generally take thought about the morrow, in which no work can be done any more than in yesterday. The Holy Present!

[284]   *Lebensraum*

It is only in Him that the soul has room. In knowing Him is life and its gladness. The secret of your own heart you can never know; but you can know Him who knows its secret.

[285]   *Nature*

If the flowers were not perishable, we should cease to contemplate their beauty, either blinded by the passion for hoarding the bodies of them, or dulled by the hebetude of commonplaceness that the constant presence of them would occasion. To compare great things with small, the flowers wither, the bubbles break, the clouds and sunsets pass, for the very same holy reason (in the degree of its application to them) for which the Lord withdrew from His disciples and ascended again to His Father—that the Comforter, the Spirit of Truth, the Soul of things, might come to them and abide with them, and so, the Son return, and the Father be revealed. The flower is not its loveliness, and its loveliness we must love, else we shall only treat them as flower-greedy children, who gather and gather, and fill hands and baskets from a mere desire of acquisition.

[286]   *For Parents*

A parent must respect the spiritual person of his child, and approach it with reverence, for that too looks the Father in the face and has an audience with Him into which no earthly parent can enter even if he dared to desire it.

[287]   *Hoarding*

The heart of man cannot hoard. His brain or his hand may gather into its box and hoard, but the moment the thing has passed into the box, the heart has lost it and is hungry again. If a man would *have,* it is the Giver he must have; . . . Therefore all that He makes must be free to come and go through the heart of His child; he can enjoy it only as it passes, can enjoy only its life, its soul, its vision, its meaning, not itself.

[288] *Today and Yesterday*

This day's adventure, however, did not turn out like yesterday's, although it began like it; and indeed today is very seldom like yesterday, if people would note the differences. . . . The princess ran through passage after passage, and could not find the stair of the tower. My own suspicion is that she had not gone up high enough, and was searching on the second instead of the third floor.

[289] *Obstinate Illusion*

He jumped up, as he thought, and began to dress, but, to his dismay, found that he was still lying in bed. "Now then I will!" he said. "Here goes! I *am* up now!" But yet again he found himself snug in bed. Twenty times he tried, and twenty times he failed; for in fact he was not awake, only dreaming that he was.

[290]   *Possessions*

Happily for our blessedness, the joy of possession soon palls.

[291]   *Lost in the Mountains*

The fear returned. People had died in the mountains of hunger, and I began to make up my mind to meet the worst. I had not yet learned that the approach of any fate is just the preparation for that fate. I troubled myself with the care of that which was not impending over me. . . . Had I been wearier and fainter, it would have appeared less dreadful.

[292]   *The Birth of Persecution*

Clara's words appeared to me quite irreverent . . . but what to answer her I did not know. I almost began to dislike her; for it is often incapacity for defending the faith they love which turns men into persecutors.

[293] *Daily Death*

We die daily. Happy those who daily come to life as well.

[294] *On Duty to Oneself*

"But does a man owe nothing to himself?"—"Nothing that I know of. I am under no obligation to myself. How can I divide myself and say that the one half of me is indebted to the other? To my mind, it is a mere fiction of speech."—"But whence, then, should such a fiction arise?"—"From the dim sense of a real obligation, I suspect—the object of which is mistaken. I suspect it really springs from our relation to the unknown God, so vaguely felt that a false form is readily accepted for its embodiment. . . ."

[295] *A Theory of Sleep*

It may be said of the body in regard of sleep as well as in regard of death, "It is sown in weakness, it is raised in power. . . ." No one can deny the power of the wearied body to paralyze the soul; but I have a correlate theory which I love, and which I expect to find true—that, while the body wearies the mind, it is the mind that restores vigor to the body, and then, like the man who has built him a stately palace, rejoices to dwell in it. I believe that, if there be a living, conscious love at the heart of the universe, the mind, in the quiescence of its consciousness in sleep, comes into a less disturbed contact with its origin, the heart of the creation; whence gifted with calmness and strength for itself, it grows able to impart comfort and restoration to the weary frame. The cessation of labor affords but the necessary occasion; makes it possible, as it were, for the occupant of an outlying station in the wilderness to return to his Father's house for fresh supplies.... The child-soul goes home at night, and returns in the morning to the labors of the school.

[296]   *Sacred Idleness*

Work is not always required of a man. There is such a thing as a sacred idleness, the cultivation of which is now fearfully neglected.

[297] *The Modern Bane*

Former periods of the world's history when that blinding self-consciousness which is the bane of ours was yet undeveloped. . . .

[298] *Immortality*

To some minds the argument for immortality drawn from the apparently universal shrinking from annihilation must be ineffectual, seeing they themselves do not shrink from it. . . . If there is no God, annihilation is the one thing to be longed for, with all that might of longing which is the mainspring of human action. In a word, it is not immortality the human heart cries out after, but that immortal, eternal thought whose life is its life, whose wisdom is its wisdom. . . . Dissociate immortality from the living Immortality, and it is not a thing to be desired.

[299] *Prayer*

"O God!" I cried and that was all. But what are the prayers of the whole universe more than expansion of that one cry? It is not what God can give us, but God that we want.

[300] *Self*

I sickened at the sight of Myself; how should I ever get rid of the demon? The same instant I saw the one escape: I must offer it back to its source—commit it to Him who had made it. I must live no more from it but from the source of it; seek to know nothing more of it than He gave me to know by His presence therein. . . . What flashes of self-consciousness might cross me, should be God's gift, not of my seeking, and offered again to Him in every new self-sacrifice.

[301] *Visions*

A man may see visions manifold, and believe them all; . . . something more is needed—he must have that presence of God in his soul of which the Son of Man spoke, saying "If a man love me, he will keep my words; and my Father will love him, and we will come unto him, and make our abode with him."

[302] *The Impervious Soul*

As for any influence from the public officers of religion, a contented soul may glide through them all for a long life, unstruck to the last, buoyant and evasive as a bee among hailstones.

[303] *An Old Garden*

Not one of the family had ever cared for it on the ground of its old-fashionedness; its preservation was owing merely to the fact that their gardener was blessed with a wholesome stupidity rendering him incapable of unlearning what his father, who had been gardener there before him, had had marvelous difficulty in teaching him. We do not half appreciate the benefits to the race that spring from honest dullness. The *clever* people are the ruin of everything.

[304]   *Experience*

Those who gain no experience are those who shirk the King's highway for fear of encountering the Duty seated by the roadside.

[305]   *Difficulties*

It often seems to those in earnest about the right as if all things conspired to prevent their progress. This, of course, is but an appearance, arising in part from this, that the pilgrim must be headed back from the side-paths into which he is constantly wandering.

[306]   *A Hard Saying*

There are those who in their very first seeking of it are nearer to the Kingdom of Heaven than many who have for years believed themselves of it. In the former there is more of the mind of Jesus, and when He calls them they recognize Him at once and go after Him; while the others examine Him from head to foot, and finding Him not sufficiently like the Jesus of their conception, turn their backs and go to church or chapel or chamber to kneel before a vague form mingled of tradition and fancy.

[307]   *Truisms*

A mere truism, is it? Yes, it is, and more is the pity; for what is a truism, as most men count truisms? What is it but a truth that ought to have been buried long ago in the lives of men—to send up forever the corn of true deeds and the wine of loving kindness—but, instead of being buried in friendly soil, is allowed to lie about, kicked hither and thither in the dry and empty garret of their brains, till they are sick of the sight and sound of it and, to be rid of the thought of it, declare it to be no living truth but only a lifeless truism? Yet in their brain that truism must rattle until they shift to its rightful quarters in their heart, where it will rattle no longer but take root and be a strength and loveliness.

[308] *On Asking Advice*

When people seek advice it is too often in the hope of finding the adviser side with their second familiar self instead of their awful first self of which they know so little.

[309] *No Heel Taps*

It must be remembered that a little conceit is no more to be endured than a great one, but must be swept utterly away.

[310] *Silence Before the Judge*

Think not about thy sin so as to make it either less or greater in thine own eyes. Bring it to Jesus and let Him show thee how vile a thing it is. And leave it to Him to judge thee, sure that He will judge thee justly; extenuating nothing, for He hath to cleanse thee utterly; and yet forgetting no smallest excuse that may cover the amazement of thy guilt or witness for thee that not with open eyes didst thou do the deed. . . . But again, I say, let it be Christ that excuseth thee. He will do it to more purpose than thou, and will not wrong thy soul by excusing thee a hair too much.

[311]   *Nothing So Deadening*

Nothing is so deadening to the divine as an habitual dealing with the outsides of holy things.

[312]   *Rounding and Completion*

The only perfect idea of life is a unit, self-existent and creative. That is God, the only One. But to this idea, in its kind, must every life, to be complete as life, correspond; and the human correspondence to self-existence is that the man should round and complete himself by taking in to himself his Origin; by going back and in his own will adopting that Origin. . . . Then has he completed the cycle by turning back upon his history, laying hold of his Cause, and willing his own being in the will of the only I AM.

[313] *Immortality*

"I cannot see what harm would come of letting us know a little—as much at least as might serve to assure us that there was more of *something* on the other side"—Just this; that, their fears allayed, their hopes encouraged from any lower quarter, men would (as usual) turn away from the Fountain, to the cistern of life. . . . That there are thousands who would forget God if they could but be assured of such a tolerable state of things beyond the grave as even this wherein we now live, is plainly to be anticipated from the fact that the doubts of so many in respect of religion concentrate themselves nowadays upon the question whether there is any life beyond the grave; a question which . . . does not immediately belong to religion at all. Satisfy such people, if you can, that they shall live, and what have they gained? A little comfort perhaps—but a comfort not from the highest source, and possibly gained too soon for their well-being. Does it bring them any nearer to God than they were before? Is He filling one cranny more of their hearts in consequence?

[314] *The Eternal Now*

The bliss of the animals lies in this, that, on their lower level, they shadow the bliss of those—few at any moment on the earth—who do not "look before and after, and pine for what is not" but live in the holy carelessness of the eternal *now*.

[315] *The Silences Below*

Even the damned must at times become aware of what they are, and then surely a terrible though momentary hush must fall upon the forsaken regions.

[316] *Dipsomania*

It is a human soul still, and wretched in the midst of all that whisky can do for it. From the pit of hell it cries out. So long as there is that which can sin, it is a man. And the prayer of misery carries its own justification, when the sober petitions of the self-righteous and the unkind are rejected. He who forgives not is not forgiven, and the prayer of the Pharisee is as the weary beating of the surf of hell, while the cry of a soul out of its fire sets the heartstrings of love trembling.

[317] *Reminder*

But the sparrow and the rook are just as respectable in reality, though not in the eyes of the henwife, as the egg-laying fowl, or the dirt-gobbling duck.

[318] *Things Rare and Common*

The best things are the commonest, but the highest types and the best combinations of them are the rarest. There is more love in the world than anything else, for instance; but the best love and the individual in whom love is supreme are the rarest of all things.

[319] *Holy Laughter*

It is the heart that is not yet sure of its God that is afraid to laugh in His presence.

[320] *The Self*

Vain were the fancy, by treatise, or sermon, or poem, or tale, to persuade a man to forget himself. He cannot if he would. Sooner will he forget the presence of a raging tooth. There is no forgetting of ourselves but in the finding of our deeper, our true self—God's idea of us when He devised us—the Christ in us. Nothing but that self can displace the false, greedy, whining self, of which most of us are so fond and proud. And that self no man can find for himself . . . "but as many as received Him, to them gave He power to become the sons of God."

[321] *Either–Or*

Of all teachings that which presents a far distant God is the nearest to absurdity. Either there is none, or He is nearer to every one of us than our nearest consciousness of self.

[322]   *Prayer*

So thinking, she began to pray to what dim, distorted reflection of God there was in her mind. They alone pray to the real God, the Maker of the heart that prays, who know His son Jesus. If our prayers were heard only in accordance with the idea of God to which we seem to ourselves to pray, how miserably would our infinite wants be met! But every honest cry, even if sent into the deaf ear of an idol, passes on to the ears of the unknown God, the heart of the unknown Father.

[323]   *A Bad Conscience*

She was sorely troubled with what is, by huge discourtesy, called a bad conscience—being in reality a conscience doing its duty so well that it makes the whole house uncomfortable.

[324]   *Money*

He had a great respect for money and much overrated its value as a means of doing even what he called good: religious people generally do.

[325]   *Scrubbing the Cell*

The things that come out of a man are they that defile him, and to get rid of them a man must go into himself, be a convict, and scrub the floor of his cell.

[326]   *The Mystery of Evil*

Middling people are shocked at the wickedness of the wicked; Gibbie, who knew both so well, was shocked only at the wickedness of the righteous. He never came quite to understand Mr. Sclater: the inconsistent never can be *understood*. That only which has absolute reason in it can be understood of man. There is a bewilderment about the very nature of evil which only He who made us capable of evil that we might be good, can comprehend.

[327]   *Prudence*

No man can order his life, for it comes flowing over him from behind. . . . The one secret of life and development is not to devise and plan but to fall in with the forces at work—to do every moment's duty aright—that being the part in the process allotted to us: and let come—not what will, for there is no such thing—but what the eternal thought wills for each of us, has intended in each of us from the first.

[328]   *Competition*

No work noble or lastingly good can come of emulation any more than of greed: I think the motives are spiritually the same.

[329]   *Method*

By obeying one learns how to obey.

[330] *Prudence*

Had he had more of the wisdom of the serpent . . . he would perhaps have known that to try too hard to make people good is one way to make them worse; that the only way to make them good is to be good—remembering well the beam and the mote; that the time for speaking comes rarely, the time for being never departs.

[331] *How to Become a Dunce*

Naturally capable, he had already made of himself rather a dull fellow; for when a man spends his energy on appearing to have, he is all the time destroying what he has, and therein the very means of becoming what he desires to seem. If he gains his end, his success is his punishment.

[332] *Love*

He was . . . one who did not make the common miserable blunder of taking the shadow cast by love—the desire, namely, to be loved—for love itself; his love was a vertical sun, and his own shadow was under his feet. . . . But do not mistake me through confounding, on the other hand, the desire to be loved—which is neither wrong nor noble, any more than hunger is either wrong or noble—and the delight in being loved, to be devoid of which a man must be lost in an immeasurably deeper, in an evil, ruinous, yea, a fiendish selfishness.

[333] *Preacher's Repentance*

O Lord, I have been talking to the people;
Thought's wheels have round me whirled a fiery zone,
And the recoil of my word's airy ripple
My heart heedful has puffed up and blown.
Therefore I cast myself before thee prone:
Lay cool hands on my burning brain and press
From my weak heart the swelling emptiness.

[334] *Deeds*

I would *go* near thee—but I cannot press

Into thy presence—it helps not to presume.
Thy doors are deeds.

[335]   *Prayer*

My prayers, my God, flow from what I am not;
I think thy answers make me what I am.
Like weary waves thought follows upon thought,
But the still depth beneath is all thine own,
And there thou mov'st in paths to us unknown.
Out of strange strife thy peace is strangely wrought;
If the lion in us pray—thou answerest the lamb.

[336]   *The House Is Not for Me*

The house is not for me—it is for Him.
His royal thoughts require many a stair,
Many a tower, many an outlook fair
Of which I have no thought.

[337] *Hoarding*

In holy things may be unholy greed.
Thou giv'st a glimpse of many a lovely thing
Not to be stored for use in any mind,
But only for the present spiritual need.
The holiest bread, if hoarded, soon will breed
The mammon-moth, the having pride. . . .

[338] *The Day's First Job*

With every morn my life afresh must break
The crust of self, gathered about me fresh.

[339] *Obstinate Illusion*

Have pity on us for the look of things,
When blank denial stares us in the face.
Although the serpent mask have lied before
It fascinates the bird.

[340]   *The Rules of Conversation*

Only no word of mine must ever foster
The self that in a brother's bosom gnaws;
I may not fondle failing, nor the boaster
Encourage with the breath of my applause.

[341]   *A Neglected Form of Justice*

We should never wish our children or friends to do
what we would not do ourselves if we were in their
positions. We must accept righteous sacrifices as well as
make them.

[342]   *Good*

"But if a body was never to do anything but what he
knew to be good, he would have to live half his time
doing nothing" — "How little you must have thought!
Why, you don't seem even to know the good of the
things you are constantly doing. Now don't mistake
me. I don't mean you are good for doing them. It is a
good thing to eat your breakfast, but you don't fancy

it's very good of you to do it. The thing is good—not you. . . . There are a great many more good things than bad things to do."

[343] *Thou Shalt Not Make Any Graven Image*

"Could you not give me some sign, or tell me something about you that never changes, or some other way to know you, or thing to know you by?"—"No, Curdie: that would be to keep you from knowing me. You must know me in quite another way from that. It would not be the least use to you or me either if I were to make you know me in that way. It would be but to know the sign of me—not to know me myself."

[344] *How to Become a Dunce*

A beast does not know that he is a beast, and the nearer a man gets to being a beast the less he knows it.

[345] *Our Insolvency*

If we spent our lives in charity, we should never over-take neglected claims — claims neglected from the very beginning of the relations of men.

[346] *A Sad Pity*

"If ever I prayed, mother, I certainly have not given it up." — "Ever prayed, Ian! When a mere child you prayed like an aged Christian!" — "Ah, mother, that was a sad pity! I asked for things of which I felt no need. I was a hypocrite. I ought to have prayed like a little child."

[347] *On Method*

"Can a conscience ever get too fastidious, Ian?" — "The only way to find out is always to obey it."

[348] *Wishing*

She sometimes wished she were good; but there are thousands of wandering ghosts who would be good if they might without taking trouble; the kind of goodness they desire would not be worth a life to hold it.

[349] *Fear*

Until a man has love, it is well he should have fear. So long as there are wild beasts about, it is better to be afraid than secure.

[350] *The Root of All Rebellion*

It is because we are not near enough to Thee to partake of thy liberty that we want a liberty of our own different from thine.

[351] *Two Silly Young Women*

They had a feeling, or a feeling had them, till another feeling came and took its place. When a feeling was there, they felt as if it would never go; when it was gone they felt as if it had never been; when it returned, they felt as if it had never gone.

[352] *Hospitality*

I am proud of a race whose social relations are the last upon which they will retrench, whose latest yielded pleasure is their hospitality. It is a common feeling that only the *well-to-do* have a right to be hospitable. The ideal flower of hospitality is almost unknown to the rich; it can hardly be grown save in the gardens of the poor; it is one of their beatitudes.

[353] *Boredom*

It is not the banished demon only that wanders seeking rest, but souls upon souls in ever growing numbers. The world and Hades swarm with them. They long after a repose that is not mere cessation of labor; there is a positive, an active rest. Mercy was only beginning to seek it, and that without knowing what it was she needed. Ian sought it in silence with God; she in crepitant intercourse with her kind. Naturally ready to fall into gloom, but healthy enough to avoid it, she would rush at anything to do—not to keep herself from thinking, for she had hardly begun to think, but to escape that heavy sense of non-existence, that weary and restless want which is the only form life can take to the yet unliving.

[354]   *Counting the Cost*

I am sometimes almost terrified at the scope of the demands made upon me, at the perfection of the self-abandonment required of me; yet outside of such absoluteness can be no salvation. In God we live every commonplace as well as most exalted moment of our being. To trust in *Him* when no need is pressing, when things seem going right of themselves, may be harder than when things seem going wrong.

[355] *Realism*

It is when we are most aware of the *factitude* of things that we are most aware of our need of God, and most able to trust in Him. . . . The recognition of inexorable reality in any shape, or kind, or way, tends to rouse the soul to the yet more real, to its relations with higher and deeper existence. It is not the hysterical alone for whom the great dash of cold water is good. All who dream life instead of living it, require some similar shock.

[356] *Avarice*

"Did you ever think of the origin of the word *Avarice?*"—"No."—"It comes—at least it seems to me to come—from the same root as the verb *have*. It is the desire to call *things* ours—the desire of company which is not of our kind—company such as, if small enough, you would put in your pocket and carry about with you. We call the holding in the hand, or the house, or the pocket, or the power, *having:* but things so held cannot really be had; *having* is but an illusion in regard to *things*. It is only what we can be *with* that we really possess—that is, what is of our kind, from God to the lowest animal partaking of humanity."

[357]   *The Lobster Pot*

She had not learned that the look of things as you go, is not their look when you turn to go back; that with your attitude their mood will have altered. Nature is like a lobster pot: she lets you easily go on, but not easily return.

[358]   *The First Meeting*

And all the time it was God near her that was making her unhappy. For as the Son of Man came not to send peace on the earth but a sword, so the first visit of God to the human soul is generally in a cloud of fear and doubt, rising from the soul itself at His approach. The sun is the cloud dispeller, yet often he must look through a fog if he would visit the earth at all.

[359] *Reminder*

Complaint against God is far nearer to God than indifference about Him.

[360] *The Wrong Way with Anxiety*

All the morning he was busy ... with his heart in trying to content himself beforehand with whatever fate the Lord might intend for him. As yet he was more of a Christian philosopher than a philosophical Christian. The thing most disappointing to him he would treat as the will of God for him, and try to make up his mind to it, persuading himself it was the right and best thing— as if he knew it (to be) the will of God. He was thus working in the region of supposition and not of revealed duty: in his own imagination, and not in the will of God.... There is something in the very presence and actuality of a thing to make one able to bear it; but a man may weaken himself for bearing what God intends him to bear, by trying to bear what God does not intend him to bear.... We have no right to school ourselves to an imaginary duty. When we do not know, then what he lays upon us is *not to know.*

[361]   *Deadlock*

We are often unable to tell people what they *need* to know, because they *want* to know something else.

[362]   *Solitude*

I began to learn that it was impossible to live for oneself even, save in the presence of others—then, alas, fearfully possible. Evil was only through good; selfishness but a parasite on the tree of life.

[363]   *Death*

You will be dead so long as you refuse to die.

[364]   *The Mystery of Evil*

The darkness knows neither the light nor itself; only the light knows itself and the darkness also. None but God hates evil and understands it.

[365] *The Last Resource*

"Lilith," said Mara, "you will not sleep, if you lie there a thousand years, until you have opened your hand and yielded that which is not yours to give or to withhold." "I cannot," she answered, "I would if I could, for I am weary, and the shadows of death are gathering about me." — "They will gather and gather, but they cannot infold you while yet your hand remains unopened. You may think you are dead, but it will only be a dream; you may think you have come awake, but it will still be only a dream. Open your hand, and you will sleep indeed — then wake indeed." — "I am trying hard, but the fingers have grown together and into the palm." — "I pray you put forth the strength of your will. For the love of life, draw together your forces and break its bonds!"

The princess turned her eyes upon Eve, beseechingly. "There was a sword I once saw in your husband's hands," she murmured. "I fled when I saw it. I heard him who bore it say it would divide whatever was not one and indivisible."

"I have the sword," said Adam. "The angel gave it me when he left the gate."

"Bring it, Adam," pleaded Lilith, "and cut me off this hand that I may sleep."

"I will," he answered.

SOURCES

BIBLIOGRAPHY

Within and Without, a Poem   1855

Poems   1857

Phantastes: A Faerie Romance for
     Men and Women   1858

David Elginbrod. 3 vols.   1863

Adela Cathcart. 3 vols.   1864

The Portent: A story of the Inner Vision of
     the Highlanders Commonly Called
     the *Second Sight*   1864

Alec Forbes of Howglen. 3 vols.   1865

Annals of a Quiet Neighbourhood. 3 vols.   1867

Dealings with the Fairies   1867

The Disciple and Other Poems   1867

Unspoken Sermons. 1st Series   1867

     2nd Series   1885

     3rd Series   1889

Guild Court. 3 vols.   1868

Robert Falconer. 3 vols.   1868

The Seaboard Parish. 3 vols.   1868

The Miracles of Our Lord. 1 vol.   1870

At the Back of the North Wind   1871

Ranald Bannerman's Boyhood   1871

Works of Fancy and Imagination
    (chiefly reprints). 10 vols.   1871

The Princess and the Goblin   1872

The Vicar's Daughter. 3 vols.   1872

Wilfrid Cumbermede. 3 vols.   1872

Gutta Percha Willie: The Working Genius 1873

England's Antiphon   1874

Malcolm. 3 vols.   1875

The Wise Woman, a Parable   1875

Thomas Wingfold, Curate. 3 vols.   1876

St. George and St. Michael. 3 vols.   1876

Exotics: A Translation (in verse) of the
    Spiritual Songs of Novalis, the Hymn Book of
    Luther and Other Poems from the German
    and Italian   1876

The Marquis of Lossie. 3 vols.   1877

Sir Gibbie. 3 vols.   1879

Paul Faber, Surgeon. 3 vols.   1879

A Book of Strife, in the Form of the Diary of
    an Old Soul   1880

Mary Marston. 3 vols.   1881

Castle Warlock, a Homely Romance. 3 vols. 1882

Weighed and Wanting. 3 vols.   1882

The Gifts of the Christ Child, and
    Other Tales. 2 vols.   1882

Afterwards published with title of
    Stephen Archer and Other Tales. 1 vol.   n.d.

Orts   1882

Donal Grant. 3 vols.   1883

A Threefold Cord. Poems by Three Friends,
    edited by George MacDonald   1883

The Princess and Curdie   1883

The Tragedie of Hamlet—with a study of
    the text of the Folio of 1623   1885

What's Mine's Mine. 3 vols.   1886

Home Again, a Tale. 1 vol.   1887

The Elect Lady. 1 vol.   1888

Cross Purposes, and The Shadows:
    Two Fairy Stories (reprinted from
    Dealings with the Fairies)   1886

A Rough Shaking, a Tale   1890

The Light Princess and Other Fairy Stories
    (reprinted from *Dealings with the Fairies*)   1890

There and Back. 3 vols.   1891

The Flight of the Shadow. 1 vol.   1891

A Cabinet of Gems, cut and polished by
    Sir Philip Sidney, now for their more radiance
    presented without their setting by
    George MacDonald   1891

The Hope of the Gospel   1892

Heather and Snow. 2 vols.   1893

Lilith, a Romance. 1 vol.   1895

Rampolli: Growths from a Long-planted Root,
    being translations chiefly from the German,
    along with A Year's Diary of an Old Soul
    (poems)   1897

Salted with Fire, a Tale. 1 vol.   1897

Poetical Works of George MacDonald. 2 vols.   1893

The Portent and Other Stories (reprints)   n.d.

Fairy Tales of George MacDonald (reprints)   1904

Scotch Songs and Ballads (reprints)   1893

MORE C. S. LEWIS CLASSICS

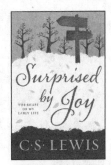

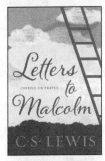

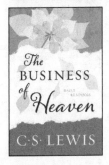

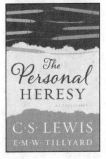

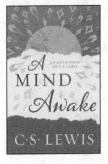

MORE C. S. LEWIS CLASSICS

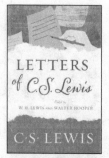

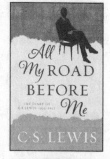